Applied Music Theory For Managers, Engineers, Producers and Artists (MEPAs)

2nd Edition
Kimo Williams

ISBN-978-0-9711360-0-7

The publisher offers special discounts on bulk orders of this workbook.
For information, please contact:
One Omik Music
41 East 8th Street, #2505
Chicago Ill, 60605

or e-mail: lbm@omik.com

Senior Editor - **Catherine Boger**
Layout and Design - **One Omik Music**
Cover Art - **Stephen Smith**
Printer - **Omni Press**, Wisconsin Illinois

Printed in the Untied States of America

Table of Contents

Preface

Why would one want to venture into the vast maze of the Music Industry without understanding what makes the Industry come alive: Music itself?

Music and the activities that make it a viable product are inseparable, but not essential to each other. In other words, an engineer can capture music without any awareness as to how the music is written; a producer can manipulate the ambient nature of a recording without knowing anything about music theory; and a manager can steer his clients' careers without having any practical knowledge of how the music is played. But why?

Like many of you reading this book, I have always had an interest in music. My start in recording technology came when I took a cheap reel-to-reel portable tape deck to my first professional concert to record Jimi Hendrix in Hawaii in 1969 . This was the start of my commitment to music and later in life the documentation of music through technology.

At Berklee College of Music in Boston I studied music composition; all students there past and present study music theory. Student recording engineers I worked with were able to follow a musical score. Artists could follow my directions in areas of tempo, intonation, and groove. As a manager of a local band, my musical opinions were credible and I could communicate them effectively because of my knowledge of music theory. Working in a musical environment was pretty smooth using the language of music, which we all spoke.

When I produced my first CD, I was surprised to find that there were not many recording engineers who had even a basic knowledge of music and its theoretical application. I did not want to sit in a control room giving musical directions to the musicians and then translating my directions to the engineer — in effect doubling my efforts unnecessarily. Time is money! It was a long search before I finally found a good engineer who also had a musical background.

At Columbia College Chicago, I created a course called Record Production for Musicians. The class taught musicians to understand the dynamics of the recording environment and the roles of those involved in it. It was during these classes that I realized Sound

Department students (engineers-to-be) had no understanding of basic music theory. They didn't know a G clef from a dynamic marking. This made the sessions chaotic at times. It seemed logical that these engineers who may not have a formal music training background, do need to understand basic music theory concepts. However, most academic music curricula require students to take Theory I to prepare for Theory II, then move to Theory III, and so on.

These and other core music classes can take two years or more. This approach to obtaining practical knowledge is thorough and important for many musicians. But such in-depth study is not a requirement in order for the Manager, Engineer, Producer, or Artist (MEPA) to be effective in a music environment. To address this I developed a course at Columbia College called Music Theory for Engineers to fill the need for music theory training that was directly useful to the MEPA. This book was created from the concepts developed in that course. It provides practical music theory that can be applied immediately in the activities associated with the creation, recording and exploitation of music. The information in it is general; complex details of music theory are omitted where possible.

The study of music theory is a long one and not a utility to be applied without understanding. However, music can also be considered a language. The syntax and written symbols can be learned and understood, allowing communication between those who understand the language to some degree — much as when one travels to another country and learns enough of the language to insure one's needs and wants are met. A language cannot be spoken fluently without having studied it for many years. The language of music is no different. This book will help you begin to understand the foreign language of music and use it to communicate effectively in musical environments.

Acknowledgements

I first want to thank my life partner, Carol, and my daughter, Beckie, for their insight in the development of this book. They were instrumental in the contextual decisions that were made. I also want to thank them both for their love and support of all my artistic visions over the years. I love you both so very dearly.

I want to acknowledge the following individuals for their contributions to this book:

Jonathan Feist for his consultation from the 1st edition through the development of the 2nd. Michael Brecker my dear departed friend for pushing me to do this book when we both realized during a recording session that such a book needed to be written. Also, a special thank you to Michael Harris who did a truly awesome proofing in a very short amount of time.

Lastly, a very special thank you to Catherine Boger for her meticulous editing and her many suggestions for clarity of content. Under quite trying times she stayed focused on our goals and helped me see this book to fruition.

Introduction

The study of the theory of music is – and should be – a long road for those looking for a professional artistic career in music. This book is not for them. It is designed for those who need a basic understanding of music to empower and improve their work in the business of music. The material is appropriate for the musical beginner or the seasoned professional who has never had the chance to study music theory. The information is designed to be immediately applicable to the work of music managers, recording engineers, music producers and music artists.

How to use this book
This book is divided into seven chapters and twelve lessons. Each lesson presents new material, then has exercises to help reinforce the information presented.

Approach lessons methodically. Do all exercises. Listen to all audio examples, repeatedly if necessary, even if you feel you understand the written word. If an audio track relates to a particular graphic, listen to the audio at least once while reading/examining the graphic. Making the connection between what you hear and what is written is a big part of studying music theory. Make sure you complete each lesson before continuing to the next.

Words in italics indicate a word being introduced; These italicized words are followed by definitions in the text, for example: *Rhythm* – how time is divided within the beat of the music.

The back of this book has a glossary with definitions of additional musical terms that may be helpful for the reader to understand. Practical information in the appendixes includes a step-by-step section on setting up a score for a recording session and answers to the practical exercises for each lesson.

Many songs are mentioned in the text; their copyright dates, writers information and musical descriptions are included in Appendix C. Additional songs are listed so that you can connect the terms you learn with songs from the last 50 years. In addition to being part of the history of the music industry, these songs were chosen for musical characteristics discussed in the lessons.

If you have already been involved in music, these lessons will reinforce the musical knowledge that is already inside you. It will give descriptive words to concepts you already hear and feel.

Take this workbook learning process seriously. Set specific study times. If you are learning on your own, you must take the responsibility of teaching yourself. You can move at your own pace, just remember to move. Above all, if you love music as I do, and are passionate – I mean truly passionate – about it, nothing will stop you from obtaining the knowledge to better serve that passion.

Kimo Williams
Chicago 2008

rhythm, the rhyme of the lyric, and the beat. The beat is even more emphasized and intensified than in other popular styles. Rap is unique among popular genres in that there may be little or no harmonic content in the accompaniment, and the melodic line is secondary to the lyric and the groove.

Track 3: Rap music

- *Top 40 Pop Music*
  Top 40, commonly called *pop*, is really a radio format that is somewhat a mix of the styles mentioned above. In fact, many of the songs on Top 40 radio are from a variety of genres. During different years or decades, Top 40 *play lists* (radio stations' lists of songs they will play on air) may include a little more rock, R&B, country, or rap. There are, however, songs labeled *mainstream pop* that hit only the Top 40 charts. The subject matter of Top 40 songs is generally light and focuses on love and romance. Some say pop music is the "least offensive to the greatest number of people," or that it is less edgy than rock or hip-hop. Whatever it is, it sells, because many people like it and will pay for it. Pop is centered on the singer. Instruments include a rhythm section with guitars or keyboards. This genre's arrangements often include layers of other instruments; which ones vary widely from artist to artist and from decade to decade. Sometimes extra guitars, horns, string sections, or loops á la rap or electronica artists are used. Producers are very important in pop. A slick, current sound is key for mainstream pop artists.

Track 4: Pop music

Other Genres

There are many other genres which we will not cover in this book but which are related to current popular and jazz styles. A few include Latin music, reggae, and musical theater. See the glossary for brief definitions of these genres.

Some mention should also be made of *traditional* genres, as they are often the roots of contemporary styles. Traditional styles include blues, folk, gospel, spirituals, hymns, bluegrass, and "world" music (folk music from other, usually non-western countries). They are of-the-people styles that have endured—sometimes for centuries—and continue to be played and written by devoted followers. Songs are usually harmonically and melodically simple. Fan bases are smaller and sales lower for these than for popular genres. However, many great musicians began by playing in these styles. Traditional music is influential because it becomes ingrained in culture, often in children's songs and melodies that "everybody knows."

The Composer and the Composition

Classical Composition

Though much of the classical music performed today was created a hundred or more years ago, classical music is still being written. Classical composers traditionally have formally studied composition (and sometimes performance) for years, often to the level of a Masters degree or higher. They are highly-trained musicians. Composers generally expect musicians to play or sing the composition as written, with limited variance in interpretation.

Jazz Composition

Some jazz composers, like their classical counterparts, spend years in school studying harmony, melody, arranging, and orchestration. There are also jazz writers with varying levels of formal training, or none at all. Those with no formal training are often self-taught musicians who develop their ideas through playing. Many jazz performers write or co-write all their own material, but jazz also has an established tradition of using what are known as *standards*, or *jazz standards*. These are songs that are widely known, appreciated and re-worked by jazz and other musicians. Some standards were originally musical theater songs ("show tunes," especially those from the 20s – 50s), some were popular songs, and others were written and recorded by jazz artists then re-recorded, or *covered*, by others. These songs have in common a general audience appeal and adaptability to different styles. Famous standards include: "Autumn Leaves," "Satin Doll," "All of Me," Stardust," and "All Blues."

Popular Songwriting (Pop Composition)

Composers in popular genres are generally called songwriters. Though less likely than jazz or classical writers to have advanced degrees in music, a few songwriters do. Others have some academic study, while still others have no formal training at all. They may have instrumental performing or singing experience.

- *R&B Composition*
  Some artists write their own songs; others are written by professional songwriters (see pop, below) or producers.

- *Rock Composition*
  Most rock artists perform music written by a member or members of the band. However, a rock band may occasionally perform a song written by a songwriter or may cover a song, i.e., record a tune previously recorded by another artist. Bands often play together to develop arrangements that they memorize, or create a lyric sheet with chords.

- *Country Composition*
  Though there are country artists who write some or most of their songs, country acts very often perform music written by professional songwriters. Nashville, where most country music is written and recorded, has a well-established system whereby writers write for publishing houses that "plug" (i.e., market) songs to artists looking for material.

- *Rap Composition*
  A rap artist performs his or her own compositions, though occasionally songs may be co-written. An artist writes or improvises rapid, rhythmic, rhyming lyrics that are spoken over *beats*. Beats (in a rap context) are drum and percussions sounds and musical lines created by the rapper, a DJ, or a "beat making" producer. To do this, *samples* (audio clips of pre-existing recordings, often from classic funk, soul, or rock records) are layered with synthesized sounds. The samples and electronic sounds are programmed into drum machines or computer applications and *looped* (set to repeat throughout the song or for a particular song section). Additional instruments or vocal parts may be added as

the song is shaped and built by the producer.

- *Pop Composition*
  As in country music, artists frequently record songs written by songwriters, though some artists do write or co-write some or all of their songs. Many successful songwriters (in both Top 40 and country) write as part of a team, often with one writing music and the other writing lyrics. Songwriters in popular and country music are often completely "behind the scenes" in that they are not involved in the recording or marketing of a song.

The Artist

Classical
Classical musicians are highly trained to produce the best sound on their instruments, to sight-read or sight-sing, and to play in time with others. Soloists can stylistically and emotionally perform, or *interpret*, music the way the composer, conductor, or director desires.

Jazz
Jazz artists may be academically trained or they may be naturally talented with great ears and little or no formal training. Many are somewhere in between, having some private or formal instruction and also learning from other musicians, perfecting their craft as they play. The Jazz artist is a self-contained act, whether a solo artist or a group. A solo artist has a core group that he or she performs with or has performed with in the past. Artists are often valued for their ability on their instruments, their compositions, their original, personal improvisational style, or

some combination of the three.

Popular Styles
Music in popular styles is focused on the singer or rapper. Though the artist may be a band, vocals are prominent. Image and style are often as important as musical talent. Popular artists are less likely to be formally trained than their jazz or classical counterparts, and less likely to read music, though they may read chord charts (interpret chords symbols, not individual notes). Though some may study academically or take private lessons, many are self-taught. Their playing abilities may be limited to their own genre.

A philosophical debate: Are popular producers and writers trying to predict or mold public taste? Does the artist actually "create" music, or just exist specifically to satisfy the needs of the market? Is there any artistic aesthetics in it, or is everyone involved—artist, writer, producer, promoter—concerned only with creating a number one song and generating market share to make more money?

The Instrumentalist

Classical
Years of study and training mean classical musicians can sight-read effortlessly. Thus, even if a group of musicians have never met, and have never seen the piece of music they are to perform, they can play together easily. Classical musicians are normally paid union scale (minimum pay based on membership in a collective bargaining organization.

Classical music is often the undertaking of a group, whether it is a symphonic orchestra or a chamber group of four players. Even when a soloist becomes well known, that individual will have a group of musicians behind him or her. A group of classical musicians, especially a large one, will need a conductor to lead them (more on conductors and music in chapters 6 and 7). Because these musicians are trained to be precise and correct, they expect others to be the same. Anyone involved in a music production dealing with classical musicians should bear this in mind. For any business dealing one should be prepared, organized, and professional, but particularly so in interactions with classical musicians.

Jazz

Jazz musicians are often skilled on a specific instrument with improvisation as a basis for their talent. As noted above, a given player may have extensive schooling, some schooling, or none at all. Some are union members and thus receive union pay. In my experience, of the professionals who play at the highest levels, about half can read music well; one quarter read a little, and the rest do not read at all. In small group performances, reading music is not essential but helpful. But in the larger big bands, written arrangements are standard, so the instrumentalist must sight read proficiently.

For professional recordings and performances, jazz musicians are chosen based on their ability to groove with other players, their ability to improvise, and sometimes for star status. Jazz groups, often called "combos," can vary in size from a trio (often bass, drums, and either piano or guitar) to a larger band between 4 and 10 players. Combos start with a rhythm section (generally bass, drums, and either piano or guitar). Saxophone, trumpet, clarinet, and other horns are

often used as the melodic lead instrument when they are associated with jazz. Other instruments more commonly associated with classical or traditional genres (violin, harp, banjo, etc.) are occasionally used in ensembles or by individual soloists.

Popular Styles

When the "artist" is a band, as in many country, R&B, rock, or pop acts, all music may be played by band members. In the case of a solo act, however, there may be regular band members, or instrumentalists may simply be hired to play for recordings or tours. In both jazz and popular styles, players who are available for hire are known as *studio musicians* or *session players*. These musicians are not regular members of a band and are usually not famous on their own.

Studio musicians are often paid union wages. They usually can sight read music or a chord chart (the latter is more often the case for rhythm section players); the better their ability to groove with other players, follow a producer's instructions, and improve the arrangement, the more they are in demand and the higher their fees.

Rap is different from other popular styles in that the DJ or Producer (or the artist), rather than musicians, create the groove by layering samples and looped synthesized tracks. A DJ or the rapper may use a turntable to *scratch* (move a record back and forth rhythmically under the needle), adding to the groove of the music. Some artists may incorporate instrumentalists into live performances or recordings, but there are no "typical" rap instruments other than turntables.

The Audience

The Classical Audience

Fans of live classical music have often studied classical music history and forms. They are appreciative audiences who come to hear the nuances of the performance, so all sounds, from the loudest (all instruments playing and cymbals crashing) to the quietest (a soloist playing a soft passage) must be audible to all audience members. Thus, those attending are expected to be very quiet. Tradition dictates that applause is held until the end of a piece. The audience does not even clap between *movements* (long sections of a piece) even though there is silence.

The Jazz Audience

Live playing is very much a part of jazz. During a performance, jazz tradition is that each performer is recognized with applause when he or she finishes an improvised solo within the overall arrangement. Depending on the particular subgenre or artist, audience members may sit quietly, only applauding for solos and at the end of songs, or may shout encouragement. In informal settings, if a musician is in the audience, they may be asked to "sit in"—come up and play a song or two—with the band.

The Popular Audience

All popular genres vary according to artist and venue. If playing at a dance venue, musicians appreciate the audience dancing, clapping, and moving. In a concert hall or sit-down club, audience members may sit quietly and applaud only at the end of songs. Sometimes, whether encouraged by performers or not, attendees may clap or sing along, chant a response to what the singer is singing, or shout general encouragement. Physically, they may bounce, rock, or sway in their seats. Some may yell, whistle, pump their fists, and stomp their feet. Rowdier crowds may slam dance and throw objects.

Lesson 1 Practical Exercises

A. Questions

In the context of this book PLEASE ANSWER THE FOLLOWING QUESTIONS:

1. What is an artist?

2. What is the difference between *reading music* and *sight-reading*?

3. In general, what is the difference between *comping* and *improvising*?

4. What is the difference between a song and a record?

5. What is an arrangement?

When someone refers to a *style*, they might mean *genre* or *sub-genre*. What are two other definitions for the word *style* ?

6. (a)_____

7. (b)_____

What are two differences between rap songs and most songs in other genres?

8. (a)_____

9. (b_____

Name 2 traditional genres:

10. _____ , _____

Lesson 1 Practical Exercises

B. Genre Matching

Match genres with facts about them. Some answers will be used twice.

1. Classical

2. Jazz

3. Popular

4. R&B

5. Country

6. Rock

7. Pop (Top 40)

8. Rap

a. Sub-genres include bebop.

b. Sub-genres include alternative.

c. Rhythmically syncopated, harmonically complex.

d. Number 1 music radio format.

e. Maybe the child of R&B and country.

f. May be the only true American art form.

g. Lyrics can usually be heard clearly in the mix.

h. Large category including rock, R&B, & pop.

i. Child of rural European folk and the blues.

j. Blues harmony, jazz rhythm and gospel influence.

k. Audience claps during songs, after solos.

l. Audience is quiet until the end of the piece.

m. Associated with DJs in its origin and production.

n. "Art music."

o. 100% of the musicians can read music.

p. A radio format that is a mixture of other genres.

Chapter 2: Introduction to Analysis and Notation (or: Breaking it Down)

What you should know:
• How to break down the elements of a song, starting with song form
• The basics of music notation, its different uses, and limitations as used in the Music Industry

Why you should know it:
Song sections are named and used in most music contexts and are the clearest place for non-musicians to begin to analyze a piece of music. To a greater or lesser extent in different contexts, music notation is the standard tool used to communicate musical thought from one musician to another. Those who can understand music as a language will have a competitive advantage in the recording industry.

The Language of Music

Music is an abstract expression that we cannot touch, smell, or see. It can be hard—some say impossible—to define or describe. Yet we keep trying. If you've ever written out the words of a song you like, you understand the desire to capture and retain music in writing. Most people are happy to just listen to and feel music and leave definition and description to someone else. But for those who want to have an impact in this industry, that's not a choice. In the music business, music is the product. You must be able to discuss your product and break it down into all of its pieces and the "raw materials" needed to create it.

One fact that is driven home when studying communication is that *language is the first barrier to effective communication*! Not specifically English versus French versus Japanese, but in the nature of the receiver (listener) understanding what is being transmitted (said) by the sender (person speaking). All that we communicate—in written or spoken word— can be misunderstood. The same word may mean different things to different people. And, of course, different words may be used for the same concept. In any industry, and in life, the more clearly you can describe what you want, the better chance you have of getting it. The producer cannot communicate to a guitar player that his guitar is out of tune if he cannot identify the particular problem or cannot use words that the guitarist understands. True, he can say "it sounds weird" or "it doesn't sound right to me". The guitarist will then try to determine what is wrong, maybe thinking, "I sound bad? Am I playing too slow? Did I play the wrong notes? Should I have brought my acoustic instead of the electric?" This takes time and, of course, time is money in the studio more than anywhere. It is invaluable in the music business to be able to communicate and understand musical information quickly and clearly.

So, from what you've just read, communicating about music can be difficult and language itself can be a barrier to clear communication! Still, musicians through the years have developed a successful system for writing down musical ideas. This system allows flexibility in communicating musical information. To begin to understand the written system of music, we must listen to music and begin to break it down in to parts. The first step is analyzing song form.

Lesson 2: Song Form

The music industry has developed over the years based on the song. Longer, more complex works exist, and there is music from other countries that has no resemblance to what we in the United States would call a song, but we will concern ourselves with what is common in the current recording industry.

We can begin to break down a song by analyzing its form. *Song form* is the design or shape of musical material defined by the type and order of its sections. It can be viewed as a formula or pattern. However, two songs can follow the same formula and be radically different. Remember, most music in rock, pop, country, rap, and R&B use similar forms. You probably know these song forms even if you've never used these words:

Verse-Chorus
Verse-Refrain (or Refrain-Verse)
AABA, or *"Standard"*
12-bar blues

Song forms are defined by their sections, or parts. Unfortunately, the same words are used with very different meanings in different song forms, which can be confusing. Further, not every song can be described neatly by one form. Some songs have elements of more than one type and some songs can be analyzed more than one way. Here are definitions of common forms and the sections that make up each form and typical examples of each:

Verse-Chorus (or Verse-Chorus-Bridge, etc.)

Examples of this form are numerous—just turn on the radio. Famous verse-chorus songs include: "Yankee Doodle" (Traditional), "Jingle Bells" (Traditional), "Lady Marmalade" (Patti LaBelle and various others), "Smells Like Teen Spirit" (Nirvana), "So Yesterday" (Hillary Duff), "Complicated" (Avril Lavigne), "Crazy" (Gnarls Barkley), "Gold Digger" (Kanye West), and "Me Love" (Sean Kingston). Currently the most prevalent industry-oriented song form, verse-chorus songs can have any of the following sections, in almost any order:

Chorus – section repeated in a song, usually once after every verse or two. A chorus often has the same words every time it is sung, and usually contains the song's title. Frequently, a chorus is what "sells" the song—what people remember and sing along with. Any catchy (i.e., memorable) part of a song can be called a "hook" because it grabs the listener. The chorus is often the hook. Occasionally the chorus will come before the verse. Some famous choruses:

In "Jingle Bells" the chorus begins:
"Jingle Bells, Jingle Bells, jingle all the way…"

In "Lady Marmalade" the chorus begins:
Gitchy gitchy ya ya da da..

In "Smells Like Teen Spirit" the chorus begins:
"With the lights out, it's less dangerous…"

In "Complicated" the chorus begins:
Why'd you have to go and make things so Complicated?

Verse – section with a (usually) different melody and chord progression than the chorus. Songs typically have two or more verses with different words for each verse. Some verse excerpts of famous songs:

In "Jingle Bells" (Traditional Christmas song) the first verse begins:
Dashing through the snow, in a one-horse open sleigh

In "Smells Like Teen Spirit" the second verse begins:
I'm worst at what I do best

In "Complicated" the first verse begins:
Chill out – whatcha yelling for?

In "Crazy" (Gnarls Barkley) the verse begins:
I remember when, I remember, I remember when I lost my mind

Bridge – section that is musically and lyrically different from both the verse and the chorus and provides contrast to them. Some famous bridges:

In "So Yesterday," the bridge is the section beginning:
If you're over me, I'm already over you…

In "Me Love," the bridge is the section beginning:
Why ya leave me, wh-, why ya leave me…

Pre-chorus or *Ramp* – short section that provides a transition from the verse to the chorus. This section gives a sense of "leaning" or "building" toward the chorus. It "ramps up" musical tension, leading the listener's ear to the chorus.

In "Smells Like Teen Spirit" the pre-chorus begins:
Hello, hello, hello, how low?
In "Complicated" the pre-chorus begins:
Somebody else 'round everyone else

In "So Yesterday" the pre-chorus is:
Not today, not today, not today...

Instrumental break or *Instrumental* – section, often the same length and chords as the verse, chorus, or bridge, played by an instrumentalist as a solo.

Break, sometimes called *Break Down* or *Drum Break* – section wherein most instruments or loops are stripped out, leaving one or two playing, often only drums, or drums plus one instrument. Break downs are often instrumental but sometimes have vocals. Not all verse-chorus songs have all of these sections, but they will have at minimum a verse and a chorus, hence the name.

Verse-Refrain (or Refrain-Verse)

Verse-refrain is a simple song form, sometimes called *strophic* form. It has only one section: a verse. The refrain, which is usually the title, is one line (sometimes two) that repeats for every verse, though the rest of the words are different. The refrain may be at the beginning, middle, or end of the verse, but it is musically part of the verse, not a separate section. Many children's songs and folk songs follow this form. Examples include: "Silent Night" (Christmas song), "On Broadway" (George Benson), and "Blowin' in the Wind" (Bob Dylan; Peter, Paul & Mary).

Though not in "pure" strophic form, popular music's verse-refrain songs often add a bridge. Examples include: "Oh, Pretty Woman" (Roy Orbison), "What a Wonderful World" (Louis Armstrong, Willie Nelson), "Fire" (Bruce Springsteen, The Pointer Sisters) and "When a Man Loves a Woman" (Percy Sledge and many others). Famous Refrains (either before or after their verses): "Silent Night" and "When a Man Loves a Woman" both begin each verse with the title refrain, so these songs are in *refrain-verse* form. "Blowin' in the Wind" and "Fire" end each verse with the title refrain, so they are in *verse-refrain* form.

AABA, or "Standard" form

Put simply, AABA form can describe any piece of music that has one melody or section (A) that is played or sung twice, then has a contrasting section (B), then has the first section (A) played or sung again once. These sections can be any length, but in many "classic" standards, each section is 8 measures, producing a song of 32 measures total. Famous songs following this form are: "Over the Rainbow" (Various artists, written by Arlen and Harburg), "Yesterday" (The Beatles), "You Are the Sunshine of My Life" (Stevie Wonder), and "Don't Know Why" (Nora Jones). "Rudolf the Red-Nosed Reindeer" (recorded by many, written by Marks & May) is a classic example of AABA song form with an introductory verse.

Sections of an AABA tune use the terms "verse," "chorus," and "bridge," but with *very* different meanings than for verse-chorus or verse-refrain songs. There are two main sections of AABA songs:

Introductory Verse (sometimes known as "Sectional Verse" or simply "Verse") – an opening section that is not repeated and is musically different from the rest of the song. It is often slower than the chorus and may be half spoken and half sung. An introductory verse musically leads the ear to the main section of the song. The introductory verse is a carry-over from opera and musical theater and is uncommon in current music. Most jazz standards written in the 20s – 40s had introductory verses, but these sections are usually dropped in modern performances. On rare occasions, other song forms borrow the idea of the introductory verse to build drama. Examples include: the openings of "Do You Love Me?" (The

Contours), "Starting Over" (John Lennon), "Control" (Janet Jackson), and "Let's Go Crazy" (Prince).

Chorus (long ago called the Refrain) – the whole AABA pattern, without the introductory verse. Jazz musicians may call this the *head*, which means the original melody as opposed to improvised ones played in repeats of the form in a given performance.

Bridge – in an AABA song, the bridge is simply the B section.

Understanding AABA song form

You probably already have an intuitive understanding of this song form. Take five minutes to write out the words to "Rudolf the Red-Nosed Reindeer."

The Introductory Verse begins:
You know Dasher and Dancer and Prancer and Vixen

The first A section begins:
Rudolf the Red-Nosed Reindeer

The 2nd A section begins:
All of the other reindeer

The B section (bridge) begins:
Then one foggy Christmas Eve

The last A section begins:
Then how the reindeer loved him

Variations on the AABA form are described, predictably, AABC, ABAC, etc. Famous songs with clear variations on the form include: "The Star-Spangled Banner" (AABC) and "Fly Me to the Moon" (ABAC).

Twelve-bar blues

Though many 12-bar blues songs take the form AAB, this form is fairly flexible. 12-bar Blues is a particular pattern of chords at intervals over 12 bars. Famous Examples include: "Tutti Frutti" (Little Richard), "Red House" (Jimi Hendrix), "I Feel Good" (James Brown), "Gimme One Reason" (Tracy Chapman), and many—if not most—blues songs ever written.

Additional song sections

In addition to the forms and sections defined above, there are song sections that are universal and may be used in arranging any song. They include:

Introduction or *Intro* – section at the beginning of a song, often a brief instrumental. Yes, even songs with introductory verses sometimes have intros.

Vamp – repeat a short passage of music a number of times until cued by a singer, MC, or soloist to continue. Obviously, vamping is done in live performances or in theatrical music.

Outro – the concluding end of a song.

Tag ending – a piece of a previous section, often the title or last line(s) of a section, repeated, sometimes several times, at the end of a piece.

Lesson 2 Practical Exercises

A. Questions

1. By what is song form defined?

2. What is the most common song form on the radio today?

3. In terms of song form, what is a vamp?

4. In an AABA song, what is the bridge?

5. What is the difference between a refrain (in a verse-refrain song) and a chorus (in a verse-chorus song)?

6. Which song form is sometimes called Standards form?

7. (a) Describe an introductory verse. (b) In what song form is it most common?

B. (8, 9, 10) Choose three different songs (or write your own) and analyze their forms as follows:

Write out the words, dividing the song into sections as your ear hears them. If there are instrumental sections, intros, or breaks, note them in brackets in the proper places.
How many different sections does the song have? What is the form of the song?
Based on the song form, label the sections.

Lesson 3: History and Basics of Music Notation

History
In ancient times, music was a performance art. The composer and the performer were one and the same. If a certain performance was good enough to re-create, it was passed on orally from one performer to another. Thus, memory was the only way to save music to be repeated at a later time.

However, much like sitting in a circle of people and passing a difficult phrase from one to another, pieces of music that were passed down would be altered—perhaps slightly, perhaps very much. As compositions became more complex—and, perhaps, as composers and audiences became more demanding—the oral tradition became inadequate. Some way of recording musical instructions was needed.

The ancient Greeks were the first (or the first from whom we have evidence) to write down musical information over 4000 years ago. Our modern western music notation is believed to have developed more recently, within the last 2000 years. It probably started with a lyric sheet, similar to what you wrote above. Later, small marks were made above the words to remember melodic information. Early European church musicians had a system of notation to remind singers (who would already have learned the melody by ear) whether a pitch was higher or lower than the previous pitch.

Gradually, various music theorists developed more specific symbols for what they wanted singers to sing and players to play. A whole system was created. Over the centuries, both music and notation evolved. The very fact that music could be written down allowed more complex pieces to be written and passed down to future generations.

Depending on the era and the style of music, the amount of detail written down varied. Sometimes notation was minimal—a melody with bass notes and symbols for chords perhaps. With just a sketch of the music, information was a guide to the performers who were responsible for improvising the parts they played within accepted styles and patterns. This made music easier to write out and used musicians' skills to shape the music. At other times, the composer wrote exactly what was wanted and the performers read and played it that way. This allowed composers full control of the music.

Modern music-makers take advantage of both minimal and detailed music notation—and everything between—depending on the needs of the performance and the particular musicians playing. Some of the types of written music will be described below.

Note: You should try to use musical terms correctly, but be flexible. While some terms are "right" and "wrong" to trained or experienced musicians, getting the point across is the important thing. If during a session someone calls a section the "bridge" and it sounds like a chorus to you, well, neither term will make the song sound better or sell more. Just make sure you understand one another, even if it means "translating" in your head.

Basic Parts of Written Notation
Most of us have seen western music notation even though we may not have understood it. It is based on a tonal

system, incorporating a divided octave (8-note scale) with a total of twelve equal divisions (more on this in chapter 4). Music based on the 8-note scale is not universal, but is prevalent throughout the world and is sufficient for our uses.
For starters, you should be able to visually identify the "parts" of music notation:

Staff – the framework of music notation. Plural of staff is staves. The most common staff is a 5-line staff (fig. 2.1), which is used for notating pitches. Staves are divided into measures by vertical barlines (2.2). There is also a single-line staff (Figure 2.3), commonly used for percussion and teaching.

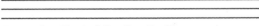

Figure 2.1: Typical five-line Staff.

Measures or *bars* – small divisions of music, separated on the staff by vertical lines called *barlines* (Fig. 2.2).

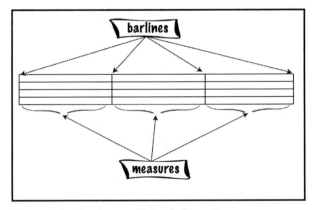

Figure 2.2: Five-line staff divided into 3 measures with barlines.

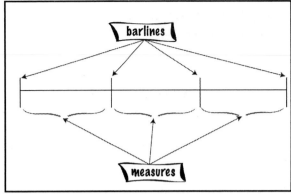

Figure 2.3: 1-line staff divided into 3 measures with barlines.

Note – a musical tone. In notation, a note is (a) a specific letter name, A – G, for a pitch or (b) a visual depiction of a note value. Notes are written differently to indicate duration—how long a note is held when it is played. Duration is measured in beats. The first few note durations musicians learn are shown in figure 2.4.

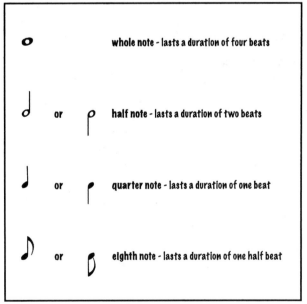

Figure 2.4: Basic note durations.

Identifying Parts of Notes

Notehead – the shape at the end of stems, or on its own. Regular noteheads are oval and are described as *open* (white in the center) or *closed* (center filled in). Noteheads' shapes are slightly slanted, "leaning" just slightly to the right, "forward" in the music.

Stem – the line that extends vertically from many notes, either above/right or below/left of the notehead. Think lowercase d or p (**not** b or q) for correct placement of stems.

Flag – a curved shape "hanging" from the end of a stem. Flags are only used with closed noteheads. Eighth notes have one flag.

Beam – When notes whose values are ordinarily flagged are in rhythmic groups of two or more, the flags are often "joined" to form straight beams. Beamed groups are easier to read than flagged groups (fig 2.5).

Note: Whole-note noteheads never have stems (no assembly required)

Rhythmic Noteheads - When music is representing non-specific pitches, such as spoken words or percussion parts, rhythm notation is often used. Open noteheads—half and whole notes—are written as open, slanted squares. Noteheads for quarter notes and smaller values are x's or slanted lines (see fig 2.6).

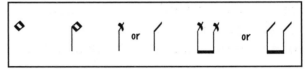

Figure 2.6: Rhythm notation. Respectively: whole note, half note, quarter note, quarter note, eighth note.

Types of Written Music

Various types of written music, some more detailed than others, are used in the music industry. Some projects may require only one type. Some may use 2 or more of those mentioned below at different stages of the same project.

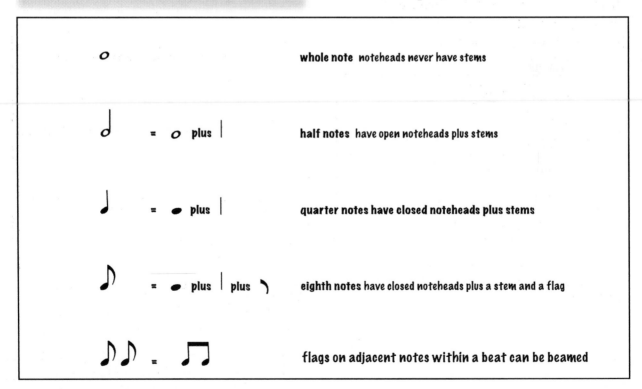

Figure 2.5: Parts and assembly of notes.

Lyric sheet – paper with just the lyrics to a song, in some cases including chords or comments, but no staff or other music notation. Many would look like the lyrics you wrote out for Lesson 2, Exercise B. Others might look like figure 2.7.

Lead sheet – music with melody on one staff, lyrics, and chords (fig. 2.8). Very commonly used by musicians. Lead sheets are what are found in fake books—compilations of bare bones music of standards or popular songs.

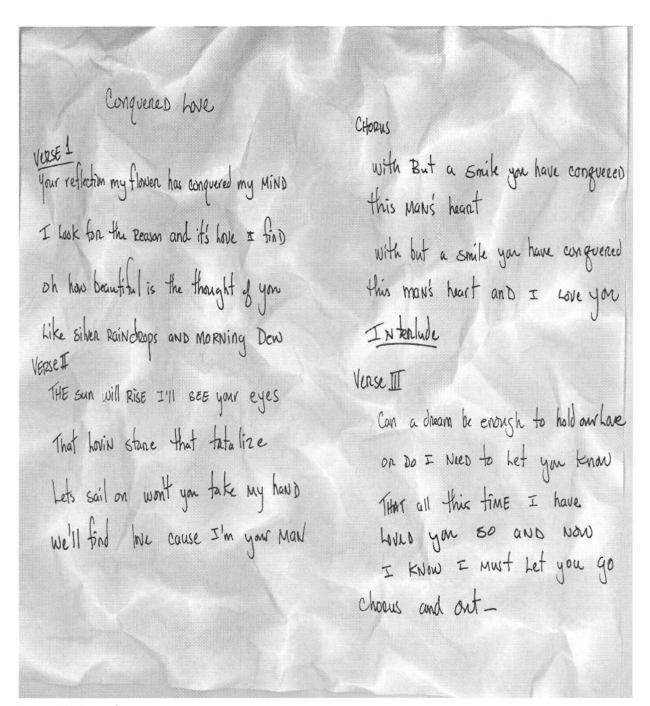

Figure 2.7: Lyric sheet.

Figure 2.8: Lead sheet.

Sheet music – (a) any printed music as opposed to audible music. (b) commercially available printed music, usually for just one song, but sometimes in books or collections of songs. Sometimes called Piano/Vocal music. Usually includes melody, lyrics, and piano accompaniment fully written out on three staves (piano on the bottom two, vocal on the top one). Sometimes include chords above the staff (fig. 2.9).

Other types of music on paper include scores (having all music for all musicians), parts (just one musician or instrument), and chord charts (a single musician's part, with chords and the outline of the arrangement, but with few, if any, notes). These will be discussed more in depth in chapter 7.

Important: If someone asks for sheet music, make sure you know what they expect. If a player wants sheet music as described in definition (b) and you bring a lead sheet (or vice-versa), that person may not be able to play.

Figure 2.9: One page of sheet music, also known as Piano/Vocal music. The top staff has vocal melody and words, the bottom two staves have the fully-written piano part.

Lesson 3 Practical Exercises

A. Questions

1. Prior to the invention of music notation, how did music get passed from one musician/generation to the next?

2. What are the advantages of having loose, general notation?

3. What are the advantages of having very specific music notation?

4. How many lines does a typical staff for pitches have?

5. What kind of note has no stem?

6. Of the note values described in this chapter, what kind of note has a flag?

7. In music notation, what is a beam?

8. Notes with stems can be written with stems pointing up or down. If the stem is pointing down, on which side of the note is it written?

9. What does sheet music (definition b) always have that a lead sheet does not?

Lesson 3 Practical Exercises

B. How many beats (total) are in the following:

1. 𝅝 = _____

2. 𝅗𝅥 = _____

3. ♩ = _____

4. ♩ plus ♪ = _____

5. 𝅗𝅥 plus ♩ plus ♩ = _____

6. ♩ plus ♩ plus ♫ = _____

7. 𝅝 plus 𝅗𝅥 plus ♩ = _____

8. 𝄽 plus 𝅗𝅥 plus 𝄾 = _____

9. 𝄽 plus 𝅗𝅥 = _____

10. 𝄾 plus 𝄼 = _____

Chapter 3: Music and Time

What you should know:
- How time is divided in music by tempo, meter, and rhythm
- How to count beats
- How to read and write basic rhythms
- Special rhythmic considerations in music performance

Why you should know it:
Music is an art that happens in time. Rhythms are written for every musician who reads music. Feeling and understanding the division of time, and ways of playing in time, are essential to making and shaping all forms of music.

Lesson 4: Tempo and Meter

Tempo
Tempo is the speed of music. One of the first instructions written at the top of a piece of music is a how fast it should be played. If we think of time passing in a steady, even series of pulses, or beats, tempo is the number of pulses per minute (fig. 3.10 a & b) A tempo of 92, for example, means 92 *beats per minute*, abbreviated *bpm*.

To help them learn to keep time, musicians use a *metronome,* a device that provides a steady, audible click on every beat. Its speed is adjustable. The second hand on a watch could act as a (non-adjustable) metronome, one that ticks at a rate of 60 *beats per minute.* In some music sequencing programs, or in studios, a metronome sound is called simply the *click*. Tempo is commonly noted as a metronome setting, such as $\quarternote$ = 105 or *mm* 105. Before reading further, use a watch with a second hand to give you a tempo of 60 *bpm*. Tap your foot with each tick. Get a feel for it and think of what kind of music might be played at that tempo. Then, using the CD for this book, listen and tap your foot to a metronome played at other tempos (or tempi).

Fig. 3.10 a & b: Time in music usually passes in a steady, even series of beats. The more beats per minute, the faster the tempo of the music.

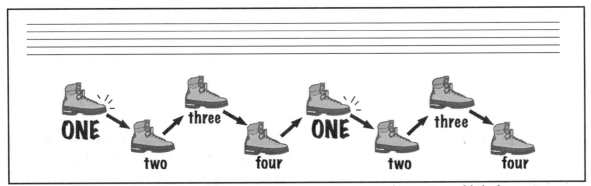

Figure 3.11: When you hear a repeated beat and accent pattern, a sense of meter is established.

Track 5: Unaccented Metronome at 80 *bpm*

Track 6: Unaccented Metronome (a) at 60 *bpm* (b) 90 *bpm* (c) 120 *bpm*

Meter

Feeling the Meter

Meter is a grouping of pulses that repeats (e.g., "one - two - three, "one - two - three," etc.). Meter is sometimes called the time of the music, as in "three-four time." Meter is easier to feel than to explain, though we will do both.

In a quiet room, listen again to Track 5 (unaccented metronome) for 30 seconds. Tap your foot with each tick. Notice how your ear unconsciously groups the ticks. Something inside your head starts counting "one – two – three – four, one – two – three – four."

In addition to grouping the ticks, your mind probably starts to *accent* (emphasize) the first beat of the group, counting ONE—two—three—four, ONE—two—three—four. The first beat in a group is called the *downbeat*. This repeated grouping of beats and accents is what we call meter. Specifically, it is 4/4 time (pronounced "four-four time") (fig. 3.11).

Track 7: A continuous repeated pulse with specific emphasis pattern.

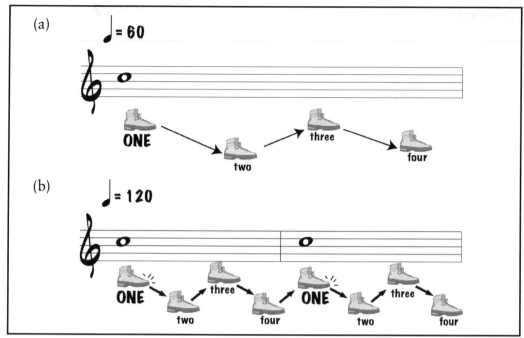

Figures 3.12 a and b: Whole notes at two different tempi.

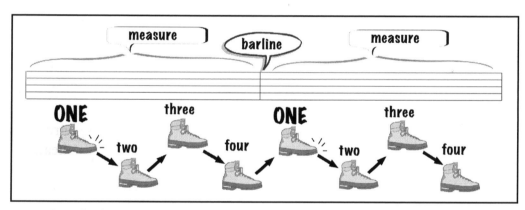

Figure 3.13: Barlines divide a staff into measures. A measure is one full "count" of a meter.

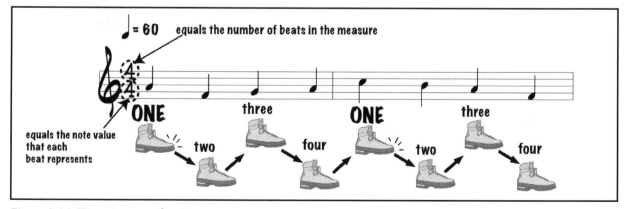

Figure 3.14: Time signature for 4/4 time.

Meter and tempo work together to determine the length of notes. Though a whole note gets four counts, the actual length of time it is held is determined by the tempo, as illustrated in figures 3.12 a and b. The duration of a whole note (4 counts) is longer in 3.12a, since the tempo is slower. Twice as many whole notes are played in 3.12b in the same amount of time because the tempo is twice as fast.

Track 8: Figures 3.12 a & b, played as written.

The meter generally continues steadily throughout a song. It is the basic "framework" of time for the rhythm of the music. To indicate that one full count has passed, we divide our music into measures, or *bars*, using barlines (fig. 3.13). Barlines make it visually easier to count and keep one's place in the music.

Meters and Time Signatures

Visually, meter is indicated using the *time signature*. Time signature is a numerical symbol at the start of the music, with two numbers, one on top of the other, resembling a fraction. Above, we were counting in 4/4, written on the staff as $\frac{4}{4}$ The top number tells the performer precisely how many beats are in each measure. The lower number identifies the value of each beat—what kind of note gets one count. For example, in 4/4 meter, the measure has four beats and a quarter note has a value of one beat (fig. 3.14).

By far the most common meter in western music through the centuries and today is 4/4. It is so common that it is sometimes called *Common Time*, and the symbol **C** can be used interchangeably with 4/4. Other meters you may encounter include 3/4, sometimes called *Waltz Time*, 6/8 and

12/8 (fig. 3.15).

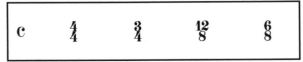

Figure 3.15: Time signatures for most commonly-used meters. The top numbers equal the number of beats in a measure, the bottom numbers indicate what kind of note gets one count.

Occasionally, there are still songs written in 3/4 in jazz, musical theater, country, and folk genres. 3/4 songs are much rarer in R&B and rock. Some examples of famous 3/4 songs include "Silent Night," "Happy Birthday to You," " The Star Spangled Banner," "Someday My Prince Will Come," and "The Tennessee Waltz." 12/8 meter was popular in the 50s.

Though now not so common, songs are still written in 12/8—especially slow ballads—in every genre. A few examples are "When a Man Loves a Woman" (Percy Sledge, covered by many others), "Higher Ground" (Stevie Wonder, Red Hot Chili Peppers), "Vision of Love" (Mariah Carey), and "Capital G" (Nine Inch Nails). 6/8 time is rare in popular music. The most famous popular song in 6/8 is "Kiss From a Rose" (Seal). There are many other meters, but they are exceedingly rare in popular genres. A few you may encounter in other genres include 2/4, 2/2, 5/4, and 7/8.

Count versus Beat

We now have enough knowledge to notate counting in two meters (fig. 3.16 a&b). (More on counting later in this chapter.)

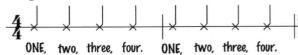

ONE, two, three, four.   ONE, two, three, four.

Figure 3.16a: Counting in four, in percussion notation.

Figure 3.16 b: Counting in three, in percussion notation.

Finding the beat of the music is fairly easy for most music lovers. Finding the count (i.e., hearing where the 1, 2, 3 & 4 counts are) may be a little harder. Popular songs in 4/4 are probably the easiest place to begin. In the majority of these songs, the snare drum falls on beats 2 and 4. If you can identify the snare (refer to Track 77 to hear different snare sounds), start counting two and four each time you hear it,—the other numbers fall into place. Practice by listening and counting along with songs on the radio, a CD, or on your MP3 player.

For practice counting in 3/4, sing a couple of the songs listed under 3/4 (above) and see if you can find the place to count (one - two - three). Songs in 3/4 generally have a strong sense of meter.

The pulse of a meter may feel different at different tempi and with different rhythms played within the framework of that meter. To complicate things, complex meters are not always counted as their time signatures would suggest.
The most common example is 12/8. Though the time signature would indicate that an 8th note gets one count and there are 12 beats in a measure, 12/8 music is usually counted in 4, with each beat divided into three eighth notes (see subdividing the beat, below). Even more confusing, 12/8 songs at very slow tempi feel like waltzes (as in 3/4).

Though we say 6/8 has six beats per measure, this meter is commonly counted

and conducted *in two* (two beats per measure, each divided into 3 eighths, like "Kiss From a Rose") or *in three* (3 beats per measure, each divided into 2 eights – less common) (fig 3.17 a & b).

Figures 3.18 a, b, and c each use the same notes in the same order. However, the meter is different in each. The feel of the melody changes because the pitches' placement in the framework of each meter changes the accented relationship of the notes. Accents are very important to the way music feels, as we shall hear.

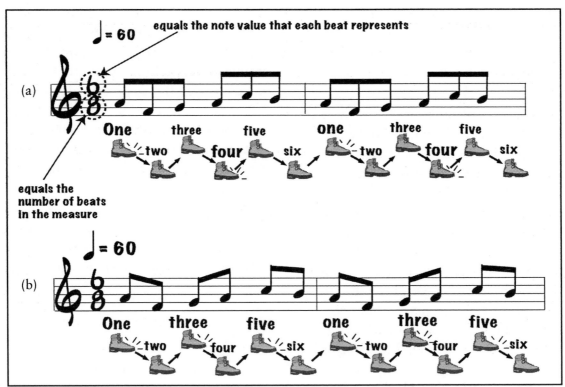

Fig. 3.17 (a) 6/8 time counted with 2 strong beats (one and four) is counted "in two."
(b) 6/8 time counted with 3 strong beats (one, three and five) is counted "in three.

Figures 3.18 a, b, and c: The same notes and rhythms when played in different meters sound different, because melody notes take on the natural accent pattern of the meter in which they are played.

Track 9: Melody played in each of 3 meters, as noted in figure 3.18 (a) 3/4 (b) 6/8 (c) 2/4.

Lesson Four Practical Exercises

A. Questions

1. What is tempo?

2. What is meter?

3. What meter is most frequently used to write songs?

B. Fill in the appropriate time signature for the rhythms below

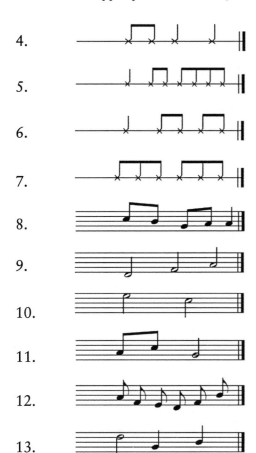

4.

5.

6.

7.

8.

9.

10.

11.

12.

13.

Lesson 5: Rhythm

Duration
Rhythm is how you divide time within a meter. You can hold a note across several measures, fill a measure with many short notes, or a play a mixture of long and short notes. We begin learning rhythm by re-examining the note values with which to divide the time. Note values are *time values*, also known as *durations*.

In chapter 2, lesson 3 you learned one of the first things that all beginning music students learn, "a quarter note gets one count." Most of the time this is true, since the majority of music is in 4/4. However,

it isn't always so. In the notation of music, *duration* refers to the relationship of a note symbol to the meter. As stated above, the meter is a framework for rhythms. While every note symbol has a given value (in beats), the actual time duration of that value is relative to the speed at which the music is played, and to the meter in which it is written. To illustrate, think about the relationship between your breath and your heart rate. The number of breaths you take is relative to how fast your heart beats (your heart beat representing the pulse of your life). If you take a breath with every heart beat, the faster your heart rate, the shorter your breath.

Figures 3.19 a & b: Both examples have beats per measure and a tempo of 60 bpm, so these would be played exactly the same.

The relationship of the pulse to the breath remains constant: one breath per beat. The same is true in music. The faster the pulse of the music, the shorter the duration of the note; the slower the pulse of the music, the longer the duration of the note. Figures 3.19 a and b are both in four, but are notated in different meters. It might be tempting to think of the melody written in 4/8 as faster than 4/4, however, the relative speeds of these written melodies would depend entirely on the tempo indications. If in 3.19a the tempo marking was ♩=96 and in 3.19b the tempo marking was ♪=96, they would be played exactly the same. Learning to count time while reading (and possibly playing or tapping) durations is important.

Tap your foot with each beat to keep the pulse firmly continuing in your head as you move forward in the music. Count off with the click, then continue. Look at the music in fig. 3.20. Listen to the examples, as the musician on the track plays the whole note, the half note, and then the quarter notes. Keep your foot tapping and keep counting.

Look at figure 3.20. Play Track 10. For each part, (a), (b), and (c), tap your foot with the count off and continue tapping and counting while the notes are played. This is a simple exercise in keeping the beat while music is playing.

Track 10: Click count-off, then (a) whole note (b) half notes (c) quarter notes, played as indicated above.

Now you sing the rhythms on Dooo (any

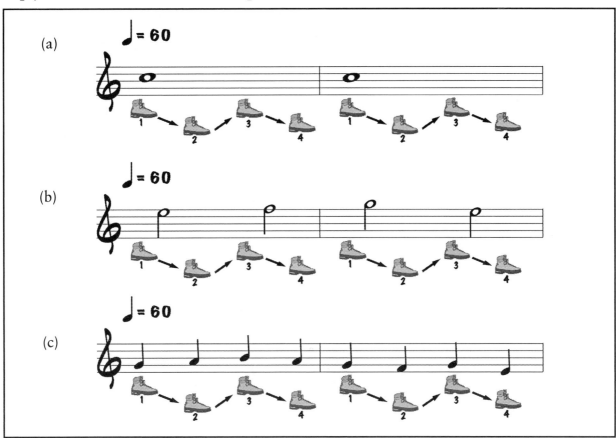

Figure 3.20: Counting measures of (a) whole note, (b) half notes and (c) quarter notes.

pitch), but with a straight, unaccented metronome track (Track 4). First establish a sense of meter by counting, then tap your foot while singing each of the 1-measure figures (whole notes, half notes, and quarter notes) at a medium tempo (Track 4). You have just performed simple rhythms of one beat or more.

Shorter Durations: Subdivisions of the Beat

The note values of whole beats learned so far are:

♩ = 1 beat, 𝅗𝅥 = 2 beats, 𝅝 = 4 beats.

Music would be very limited if only whole beats were used to write it. Shorter note values, those whose lengths are less than a beat, are known as *subdivisions* of the beat. Mostly, these divide the beat in half, then in half again.

Dividing a quarter note in half we get an *eighth(8th) note*, briefly mentioned in chapter 2. Think math for a minute: as a quarter note (one beat) is 1/4 of a whole note (four beats), an *8th note* is 1/8 of a whole note. We have determined that a quarter notes gets one count, therefore an 8th note gets ½ of a count. Remember, think math: there are two 8ths in a quarter. Therefore, logically there are two

8th notes in each beat.

A single 8th note is written with a *flag:* ♪ = eighth note (with flag ⌐), while a group of two (or more) 8ths are usually joined with a *beam:* ♫ = two 8th notes (with beam connecting the tops of stems). To count 8th notes, use the word "and" between beat numbers: "1 – and – 2 – and – 3 – and – 4 – and," but still keep tapping your feet to keep the beat (fig 3.21).

▶ Track 11: Counting 8th notes.

You have just performed two 8th notes on each beat. Figures 3.22 a, b, and c represent examples of simple one-measure rhythms that you should try to sing. Tap your foot steadily, count to establish the meter, then sing the rhythms saying "da."

Sixteenth notes are half the length of 8th notes. We need to keep the same mathematical correlation as we did with 8ths: if there are two 8ths to a quarter and two 16ths to an 8th, then there are four 16th to a quarter. As long as we maintain this mathematical relationship, subdivision is easy to understand.

Sixteenth notes have two flags: ♪. Two or more 16th notes (up to 4 in a group) are joined with two beams: ♬

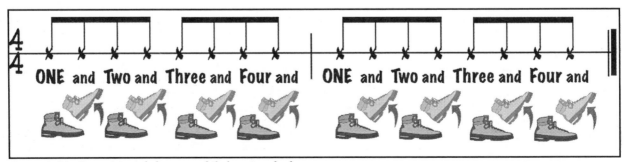

Figure 3.21: Counting eighth notes while keeping the beat.

Figure 3.22: Simple melodies.

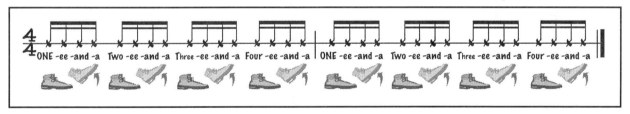

Figure 3.23: Counting 16th notes while keeping the beat.

To count 16th, notes we need extra syllables. One measure of 4/4 with a 16th note subdivision is counted "1 – ee – and – a – 2 – ee – and – a – 3 – ee – and – a – 4 – ee – and – a." Notice in fig 3.23 that the beats (1, 2, 3, 4) and 8th notes ("ands") are still in the same places in the measure as they were with 8th note subdivisions (fig 3.21, with or without notes between them.

Track 12: **Counting 16th**

Based on the divisions concept described above, a hierarchy of relative note values can be established (fig. 3.24). It is also possible to have three notes performed within the usual duration of two notes of the same value. This figure is called a *triplet* and is considered an irregular grouping, though it is fairly common in music. The duration of the triplet is equal to the value of two notes of the usual duration (see below). Triplets are always notated with a number 3 above them, sometimes with brackets, to make it clear that they are not regular 8ths, or 16ths (in

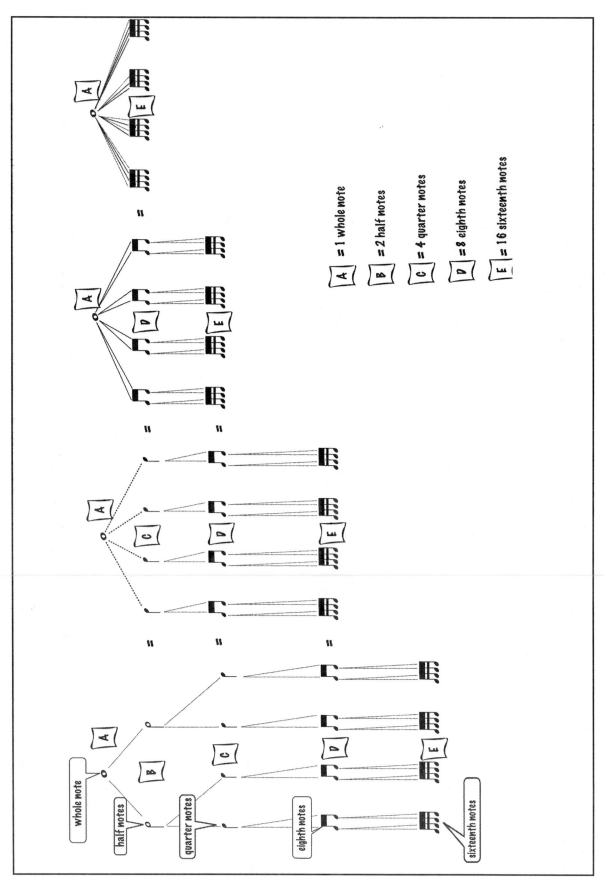

Figure 3.24: Hierarchy of note values and their relationships to each other. As in math, if A = B, and B = C, then A = C.

the case of 16th-note triplets).

♩♩♩ or ♪♪♪ = 8th note triplets, takes the same amount of time as ♪♪.

♬ or ♬ = 16th note triplets, takes the same amount of time as ♫.

There are a few different ways of counting triplets. We will use "1 – and – a – 2 – and – a – 3 – and – a – 4 – and – a" for 8th note triplets (fig 3.25).

Track 13: Counting triplets

Incidentally, we have mentioned that 12/8 time is counted in four. It can now be shown that 12/8 can be thought of as 4/4, with each beat divided into triplets rather than 8ths or 16ths. It is an ink-saving, easier-to-read way of writing it (fig 3.26).

Other types of triplets are shown in fig 3.27 a, b, c and d. Listen carefully to Track 14 on the CD to see how triplets sound against a steady beat.

Rests

In addition to notes held for specific durations, music also has silences of specific durations. For each note value,

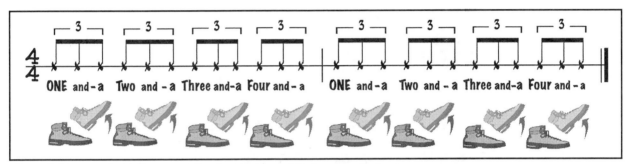

Figure 3.25: counting 8th note triplets in 4/4 time while keeping the beat.

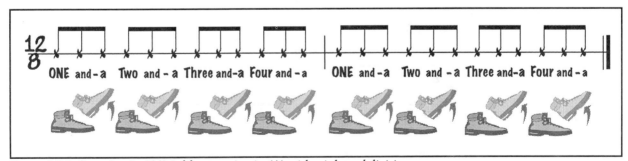

Figure 3.26: Counting in 12/8 is like counting in 4/4 with triplet subdivisions.

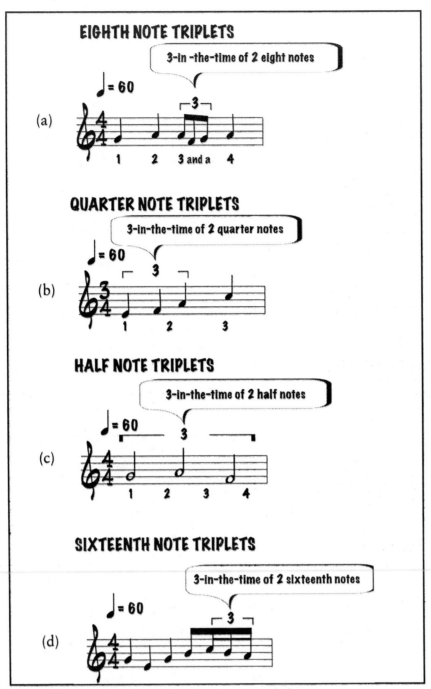

Figure 3.27 a, b, c, and d: various triplets as played against a steady beat.

Track 14: Triplets, as notated above: (a) 8th-, (b) quarter-, (c) half-, and (d) 16th-note triplets.

there is a corresponding *rest* value (fig. 3.28). A rest symbol indicates how long to be silent or "at rest." Though rests do not, of course, have pitch, they are placed on the staff. A half rest sits on top of the third line of a staff. A whole rest sits under the fourth line (fig. 3.29).

With all the choices of possible rhythms or rests, we can see that there are many ways to subdivide one measure of music. Regardless of the subdivision of the beat or the complexity of the rhythm, you

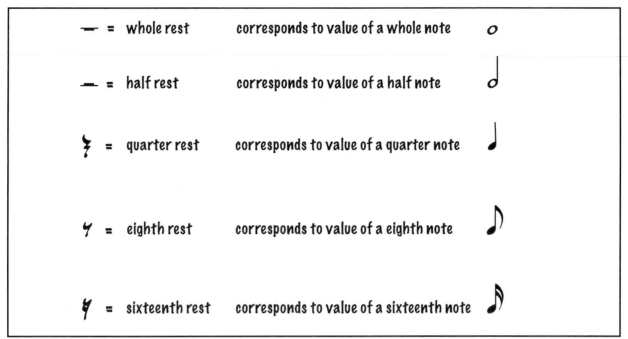

Figure 3.28: Rests. For each note duration, there is a corresponding rest value.

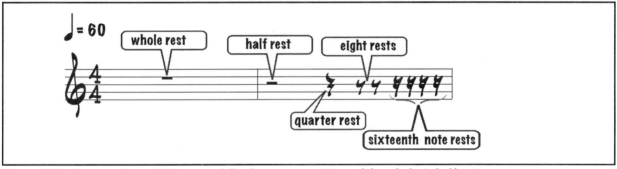

Figure 3.29: Rests on the staff. Note carefully the correct position of the whole & half rests.

should be able to keep the pulse and the correct count and still follow the music while the different subdivisions are playing.

See and hear the examples at fig. 3.30, Track 15. Listen to the count-off and tap your foot to keep the beat. Keep tapping while listening to the notes played until you are able to keep the beat (tapping your foot only on beats) while following the music.

Track 15: Three different rhythms, as notated in fig. 3.30.

Lengthening Note Values

Ties

Note symbols' durations are in multiples of two. It is therefore necessary to have additional symbols to express other values. One such symbol is the *tie*. The tie symbol is a curved line which connects adjacent notes of the same pitch. A tie extends the note's duration so that it equals the total duration of all the tied notes.

Figure 3.30: Three different rhythms. No matter how measures are rhythmically subdivided, the total note value per measure cannot be more or less than the number of beats indicated by the time signature. Keep a steady beat and you can keep your place in the music.

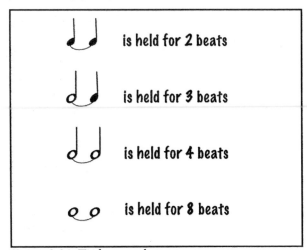

Figure 3.31: Tied note values.

Note that a tie may, and often does, require a note to be held beyond the end of the measure, sometimes called *across the barline*.

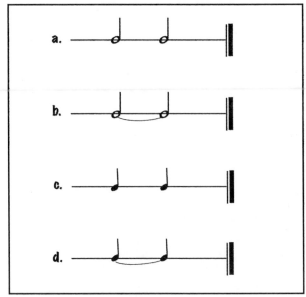

Figure 3.32 a - d: Notes that are not tied are played separately as in (a) and (c). Notes that are tied are added together as in (b) and (d).

Track 16 a - d: Figures 3.32 a – d, as sung on Doo.

Dots

Another symbol affecting note value is the *dot*. A dot placed after a note head extends the note's duration by half the value of the note. So a *dotted* half note is equal to a half note tied to a quarter note. Additional dots, when added, increase the note's duration by half of the previous dot's value (in other words, half of the half).

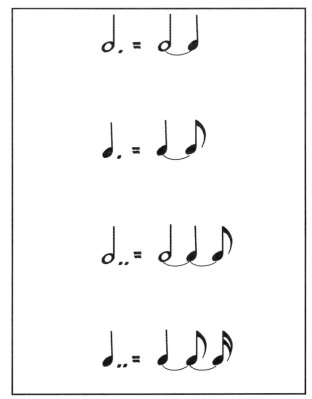

Figure 3.33: Dotted and double-dotted notes and comparable tied note values.

Note that dots can be added to rests for odd durations (not multiples of two), but ties cannot. 𝄽. or 𝄾. is o.k., but 𝄽 𝄾 is not!

Rhythm and Meter

The *rhythm* of music is how time is divided within the framework of the meter. All the different note values and subdivisions (or rests) can be used. However, the total note value in any given measure must add up to precisely the number of beats required by the meter. A measure cannot have extra beats or too few.

Rhythm also refers to how beats are accented or not accented as the music flows from measure to measure. If the accented patterns are regular and always on the beat (ONE-two-three, ONE-two-three), we say that the rhythm is metrical. The rhythm is essentially re-emphasizing the meter. The relationship between meter and rhythm can be either uniform or syncopated. In a uniform rhythm, note values and accents correspond with the time signature (or uniform divisions of the beat) and accents are placed to emphasize the meter (fig. 3.35).

🎵 Track 17: **Uniform, metrical rhythm.**

In a *syncopated* rhythm, note values can occur on fractions of beats, or accents are placed on weak beats instead of strong beats (one-TWO-three-FOUR, one-TWO-three-FOUR, etc.) (figs. 3.36 a&b). Songs accenting beats two and four are quite typical in current jazz and popular styles (Track 18).

Compare the rhythms in the different songs on Track 2; (a), the old-fashioned jazz, sounds more metrical, while (b) and (c) not only emphasize beats 2 and 4, but also have accents (sometimes called *kicks* or *hits*) that are not on beats at all, but instead are on a subdivision of the beat.

🎵 Track18: **Syncopated rhythm accenting off beats.**

🎵 Track 2: **(a) old-fashioned jazz style in a straight, metrical rhythm; (b) & (c) more typical, syncopated jazz styles.**

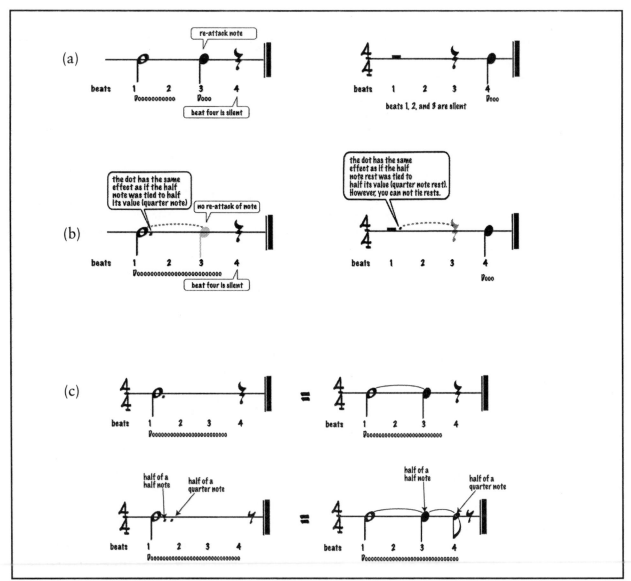

Fig. 3.34, a - c: Dotted and tied note values in a measure. Rest values in a measure.

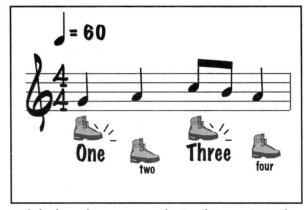

Figure 3.35: In uniform, metrical rhythms, the accents emphasize the meter's usual strong beats, One and Three.

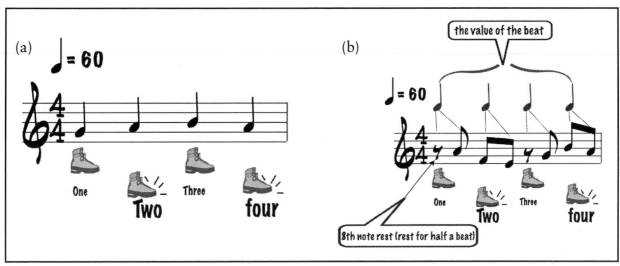

Figure 3.36 a: In a syncopated rhythm, the accents emphasize the (ordinarily) weak beats. This metric syncopation is standard in jazz and popular genres. b: Syncopation also accents off beats and de-emphasizes strong beats.

Other Things You Should Know About Rhythm

Swing

A special rhythmic consideration is *swing*. Swing refers to a way of interpreting the rhythmic subdivision of a song. Written music may indicate *swing 8ths* or *swing 16ths* to let the musician know that, throughout the piece, ♪♪ should be played like ♪♪♪ (swing 8ths), or that ♪♪ should be played like ♪♪♪ (swing 16ths). Since the notes are written identically, this instruction is vital to tell musicians the correct rhythmic feel that is wanted. *Straight* is the opposite of swing. If someone says they want a melody "played straight," they can mean either "as written" or "not swing." It is easier to hear than to explain music that swings. However, in straight subdivisions, the time is divided evenly in the measure. In a swing subdivision, the first note of the subdivision is held longer, giving the distinct swing feel.

Track 19: (a) Four measures of straight 8th notes played on high-hat cymbals; (b) Four measures of a straight-8th rock drum groove.

Track 20: (a) Four measures of swing 8th notes played on high-hat cymbals; (b) Four measures of a swing-8th drum groove.

Track 21: (a) Four measures of straight 16th notes on high-hat cymbals; (b) Four measures of a straight-16th drum groove.

Track 22: (a) Four measures of swing 16th notes on high-hat cymbals; (b) Four measures of a swing-16th drum groove.

The term swing sometimes gets associated closely with jazz due to the popularity of swing in jazz music over the decades. However, all genres have songs that swing.

Groove

Groove is difficult to define. It refers to how music *feels*. We might say it is the feel of an arrangement. Speaking stylistically, it is a pattern established by the combination of different rhythms and accents played by bass, drums, guitar, and other instruments (e.g., "a funk groove"). The hard part is describing the feeling of motion a groove gives. Everyone knows the feeling when something's grooving, but how do we put it into words?

Starting with simply counting in 4/4, we can begin to understand groove. At a medium tempo, count one—two—three—four, one—two—three—four. Once you have established a steady pulse, emphasize beats one and three (ONE—two—THREE—four, ONE—two—THREE—four). How does this feel, musically? Now keep the same pulse, but instead emphasize two and four (one—TWO—three—FOUR, one—TWO—three—FOUR). Even with a simple, metrical rhythm, the change in accent changes the feel. Now try subdividing the beat into 8ths and count, first accenting beats one and three (ONE-and-two-and-THREE-and-four-and, ONE-and-two-and-THREE-and-four-and...), then two and four. Then accent only the "ands" (known to musicians as the *up beats*) (one-AND-two-AND-three-AND-four-AND, one-AND-two-AND-three-AND-four-AND...). Notice how differently it feels when you count each pattern.

Experiment having 2 or more people tap, count, or stomp different subdivisions and accent patterns simultaneously to create different grooves. The subdivision of the beat greatly effects the rhythm and feel of the music. Popular grooves are generally based on either straight 8ths, swing 8ths, straight 16ths, swing 16ths, or triplets. Recognizing the subdivision of the beat of various songs may change the way you listen to music. See Appendix C for popular music with each of these subdivisions. Find some of the recordings and see if you can tap your foot and count subdivisions as the music plays.

Rhythmic Placement

We can and do set computers or other devices to play music with mathematical precision. Scientifically speaking, the music is rhythmically "correct," with every note in place. But the human ear (along with the feet, hips, and behinds) is the ultimate decider of what grooves. Computer-precise music just doesn't feel as good as skilled musicians playing the same parts.

Good musicians listen to each other and may play in slightly different places than exactly on the beat. The "space" around the beat, a little before and after it, is sometimes called *the pocket*. It takes practice to hear this subtle rhythmic placement. If someone is *in the pocket*, they are playing in synch with other players (even if each is playing in a slightly different place) and the music feels good. It may be said that the groove has *locked up*, or that it has *locked in*. On the other hand, musicians can play together relatively "in time" and still not create a good feeling of motion. In this case we say they're not grooving, or that the groove isn't locking up.

The feel of the groove also has to do with how closely the musicians play rhythms relative to each other. All may be playing very close to the same "place" in the beat. This is called *tight* playing. Sometimes the pocket is wider, with musicians playing in slightly different places, yet the music still grooves—it's just *loose*. In a playing situation, a musician may be told to *lay back*, that is, play later in the pocket, just after the beat, to establish a certain feel. But if someone is playing too late and not in the pocket, they (and probably the music itself) are said to be *dragging*. Playing slightly ahead is called playing *on top of the beat*, if it's grooving. If a musician is too far ahead (not grooving), they are said to be *rushing*.

Lesson Five Practical Exercise

A. Counting & Analysis

Practice counting/finding downbeats. Once comfortable with counting, go back to the songs whose lyrics you wrote out in chapter 2. Count the number of measures in every song section (Intro, Verse, Chorus, Break, etc.) of each song. In the same song, what is the smallest subdivision of the beat? Swing or straight?

B. Reading simple rhythms

Tap your foot to keep the beat while singing (or saying) the rhythms on the adjacent page. Use the syllable "da." Start slowly enough so that you can keep singing the rhythms at a steady pace, not slowing down or speeding up the tap.

Once you've tried each rhythm a few times, use the 60 bpm metronome on Track 6 to give you a steady tempo. Count off a measure or two, then see if you can tap the tempo (or continue singing on "da") in time with the metronome. Try it with the 80 bpm metronome on Track 5.

For further practice, look at simple commercial sheet music and try to sing just the rhythms of the melodies. Always remember to get your foot tapping first to establish the pulse, then count the beats for a measure or two before beginning.

1. 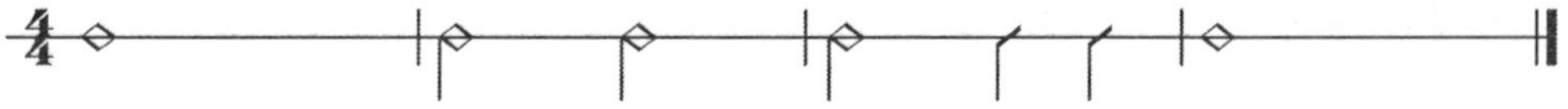

2. 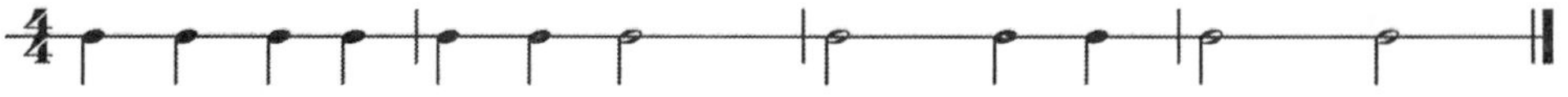

3. 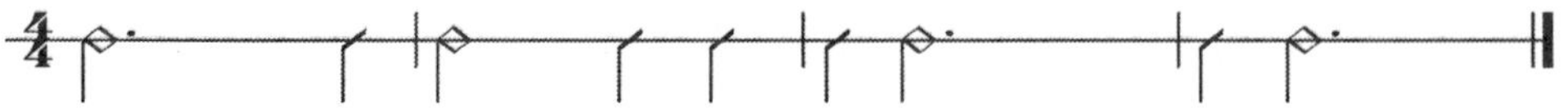

4. 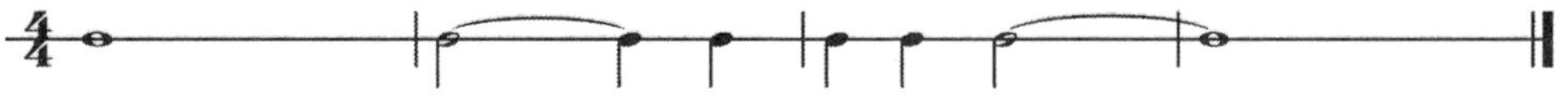

5. 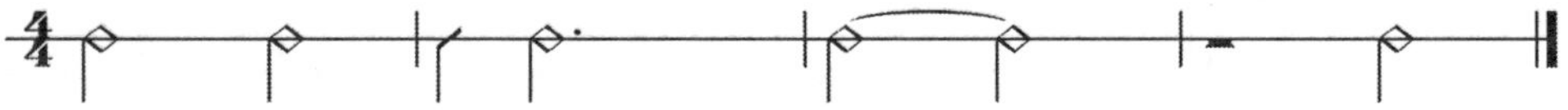

6. 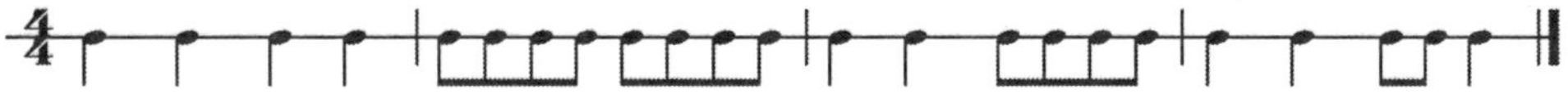

7. 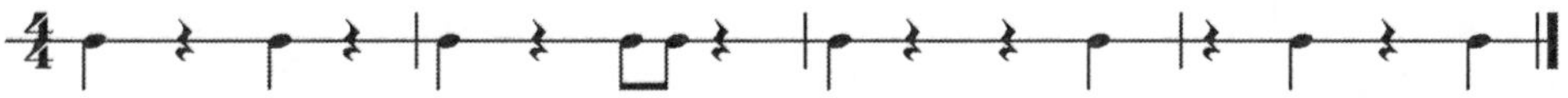

8. 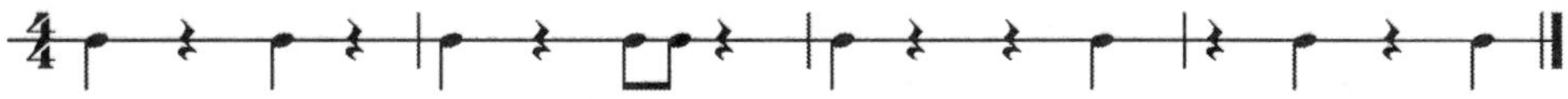

9. 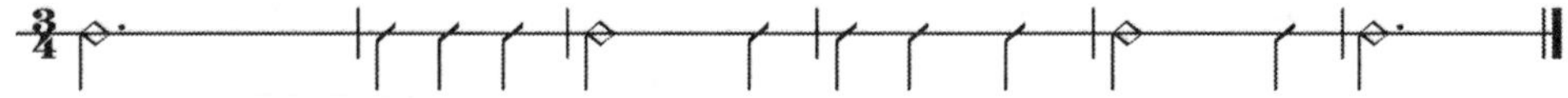

10. 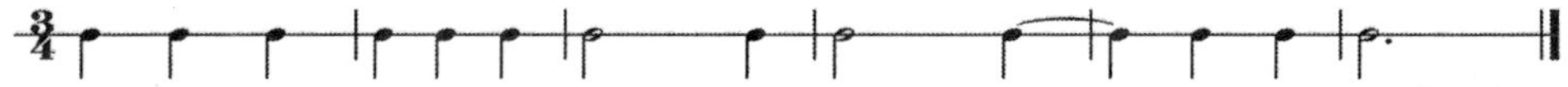

11. 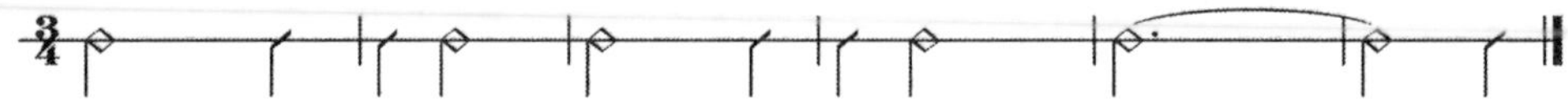

12. 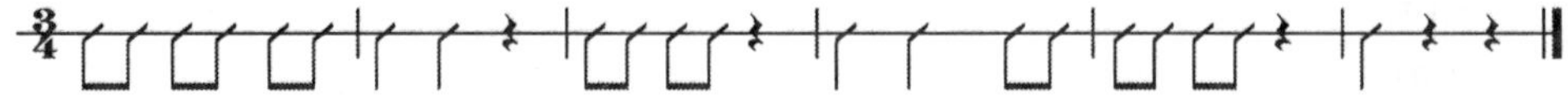

13. 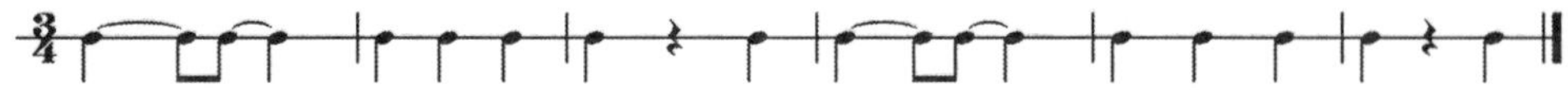

14. 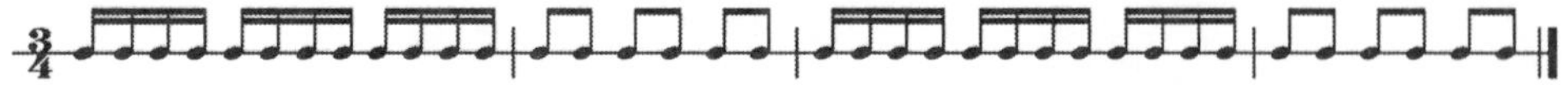

15. 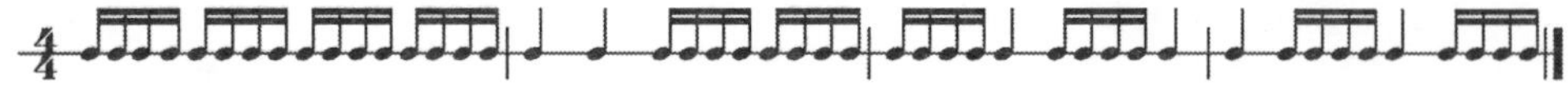

16. 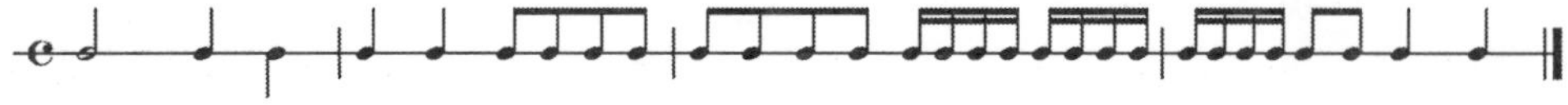

Chapter 4: Sound and Pitch

What you should know:
• The nature of sound and its relationship to pitch
• Qualities of sound and pitch and how to discuss them with others
• Basic pitch notation

Why you should know it:
In order to make musical decisions, you must have an ear educated to evaluate sound and pitch. Working in the music industry, you must be conversant with the terminology and theory of sound to understand and communicate with technicians and musicians about problems and preferences regarding sound. Pitch notation is the foundation to understanding music notation.

Lesson 6: The Nature of Sound

All sound is a result of something moving. The strings of a strummed guitar create a vibration in air; the vocal chords of the vocalist vibrate. Other instruments are bowed, hit, plucked, or blown to cause vibrations and pass the vibrations on to the air around them. Air molecules in motion generate energy that creates the basic unit of sound—the *sound wave*.

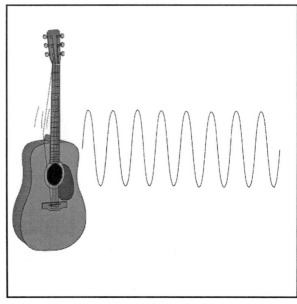

Figure 4.37: Sound is a result of motion. In this case, a plucked guitar string.

Sound waves cannot travel through a *vacuum*—a space from which air has been removed. They can only propagate through a *medium*, that is, a place in which to move molecules. Fortunately for us, the air all around us provides an excellent medium for sound to travel through. As they travel, the waves are similar in shape and motion to ripples in water. Throw a stone into a pond and observe the result. The resulting disturbance (the wave) moves through the medium (the water) in ever widening circles. Sound waves in the air cause a similar disturbance as a result of the air molecules' *compression* (bunching together) and *rarefaction* (moving apart).

How the ear hears sound

Though it may be hard to believe, the sound waves described above are not sound. Not until they're interpreted as such by the human ear and brain.
The ear is a very complex mechanism. Three basic parts that we will be concerned with are the outer ear, the middle ear, and the inner ear (fig. 4.38).

A sound wave traveling through air first encounters the *outer ear*, which collects sound and, when working in left-right tandem with the other ear, helps us determine the direction a sound is coming from. Next, the wave moves through the ear canal to the *eardrum*. The eardrum is the beginning of the *middle ear*. It is attached to the oval opening of the middle ear utilizing three bones: the *hammer*, *anvil*, and *stirrup*. These three bones, the smallest in the human body, could all fit on Lincoln's face on a penny. Collectively they are called the *ossicles*. Together, the ossicles act as a transformer, changing the motion from the air into motion in a fluid.

The inner ear consists of the *cochlea*, a snail-shaped cavity lined with membrane and filled with fluid. The cochlea is really a transducer. *Transducers* change acoustical energy into electrical impulses, or the reverse (microphones and speakers are manmade transducers). The cochlea changes the motion in the fluid to the electrical impulses our brains perceive as sound.

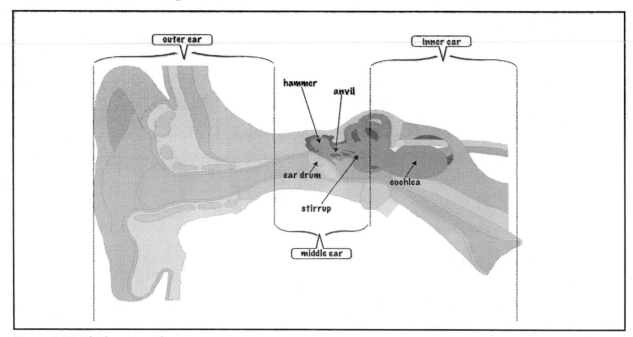

Figure 4.38: The human auditory system.

Protecting the Ear

The nerve cells that do the job of changing pressure variations into electrical impulses are very sensitive and fragile. They can be damaged by loud sounds and once damaged, they do not regenerate.

Your ears are the most valuable asset that you have in music; they're also delicate organs. If you do not take steps to preserve your hearing, you may damage it permanently, suffering hearing loss (partial or total deafness) or the misery of tinnitus, a constant ringing in the ears. It's normal to lose some sensitivity in hearing as you grow older, especially in the higher frequencies, but don't make yourself old before your time!

The body provides warning signs to indicate that the ear has been injured. Temporary Threshold Shift (TTS) is a phenomenon that occurs when you expose your ears to loud sounds. The ears' threshold of hearing moves up to accommodate these loud sounds and, as a result, you can no longer perceive soft sounds. Another warning sign is a ringing in the ears, which should subside as the ear recovers. If you have ringing in your ears after attending a concert or session, and the ringing lasts for more than a day, see a physician immediately.

Some damage occurs over time with repeated exposure to even moderately high volumes, and is difficult to detect until it is too late. Protect your hearing before you notice signs of hearing loss: use quality earplugs that reduce the SPL (sound pressure level) but not the frequency balance of the music, and keep volumes to a reasonable level.

Properties of sound

Sound has components that can be measured or described. These components effect how our ears perceive sound. The words used to describe sound often depend on who is talking. Musicians talk about the pitch, volume and timbre (pronounced TAM-ber) of a note. Scientists, who love measuring and quantifying things, measure three properties of sound waves: frequency, wavelength, and amplitude. Sound engineers may use musical or scientific terms, but will also refer to the sound envelope. As we will see, all of these terms relate to the same thing: the elements that make up the particular quality of any given sound.

Returning to the vibrating guitar string, let's look at a simple representation of the sound wave it creates. In figure 4.39, we see a graph representing a simple wave. The horizontal line represents time. The vertical line represents compression and rarefaction: a yardstick of how far the string-and the resulting wave-are moving up and down. A wave of this shape is called a *sine wave*.

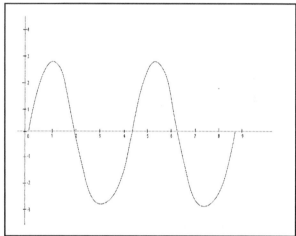

Figure 4.39: A sound wave represented by a simple sine wave on a graph. Notice that the wave passes through both negative and positive values as it vibrates.

Pitch and Frequency

When musicians refer to *pitch*, it will often be regarding a particular note name-A, B, C, and so forth. Pitch can be *high* or *low*. Musicians or singers can be *on pitch* (correct) or *off key* (incorrect; either not on a specific pitch, on the wrong pitch, or out of tune with other musicians). Scientifically, pitch is referred to as frequency. Frequency is how fast vibrations (of the guitar string, for example) occur. More precisely, it is the number of times per second a sound wave completes a cycle. A cycle is when a wave starts at 0, moves to its peak positive position (compression), back to 0, to its peak negative position (rarefaction), and back to 0 (fig. 4.40).

The number of times per second a wave completes this back-and-forth movement is called frequency. The frequency of a wave is measured in cycles per second, commonly called hertz (Hz). A frequency of 440 cycles per second ("concert A" to musicians) would be a frequency of 440 Hz. As frequency increases, pitch increases (gets higher).

Track 23: A 440, also called Concert A

Track 24: A 880, one octave above Concert A

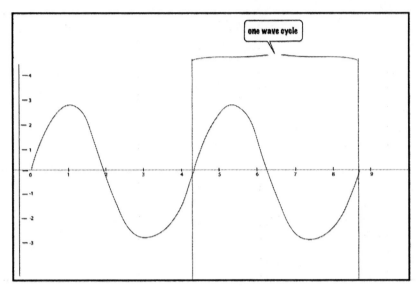

Figure 4.40: The cycle of a wave is complete when it travels from zero to peak (+), back through zero to peak (-), then back to zero.

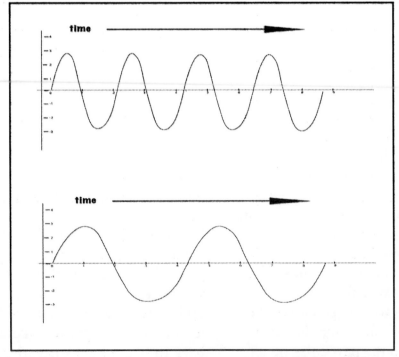

Figure 4.41 a & b: Two waves representing pitches an octave apart. The higher pitch has exactly twice the frequency (number of cycles per second) as the one an octave lower.

Wavelength

Another property of sound waves related to pitch is wavelength. The distance a wave travels to complete one cycle is called its *wavelength*. A wavelength can be physically measured. The longer the wavelength, the lower the frequency (pitch), and the shorter the wavelength, the higher the frequency. Hence, a bass playing the E string produces a longer wavelength than a guitar playing its low E string (fig. 4.42 a & b). You have probably heard of Greek philosophers Socrates and Aristotle. They and other philosophers in ancient Greece had ideas about everything under the sun. The Greek thinker Pythagoras had great impact on both mathematical and musical thinking. He developed a theory for why pitches change when the length of a vibrating string is changed. Eventually, followers of Pythagoras found that stopping a vibrating string at the halfway point created a tone that was an octave (the same note but with a higher frequency of vibration) above the fundamental, that is, the original, lowest pitch (fig. 4.43). The length of the string itself is directly related to the wavelength and frequency of the sound waves it will produce. Guitar players use this fact directly when they hold down a string on the neck of the guitar. The higher up on the neck they hold down the string, the shorter it is when plucked, the shorter the resulting wavelengths, and the higher the note.

Volume and Amplitude

We all understand something about volume. If you your favorite song is playing and you want to hear it louder or softer,

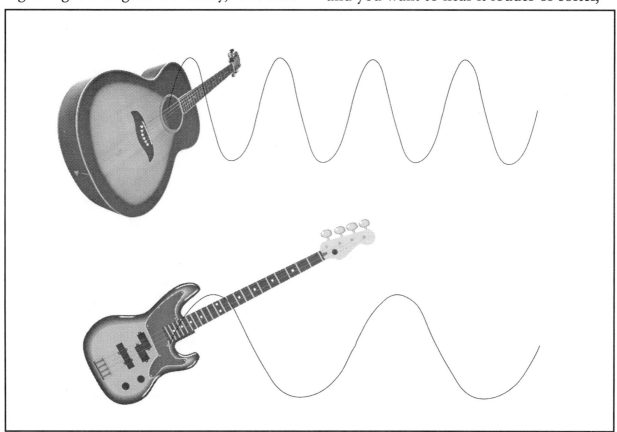

Figure 4.42 a & b: The low E strings on the guitar and bass produce different sized wavelengths. The lower the note, the longer the wavelength.

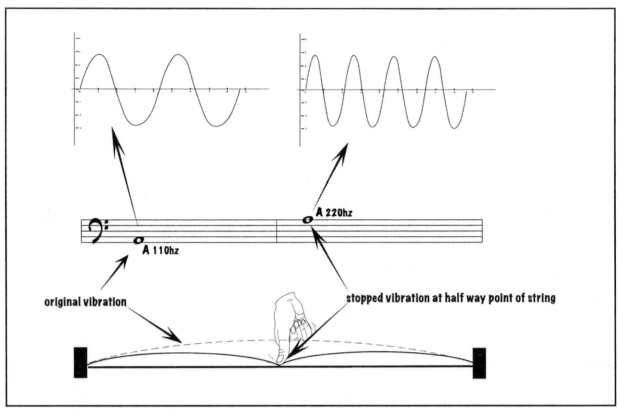

Figure 4.43 A string vibrating at its full length will sound its fundamental (main pitch, represented by the dotted line). If the string is stopped at the halfway point, a new fundamental is introduced, exactly one octave higher than the first.

you turn the volume knob so that the desired "loudness" is attained. (Note: we will refer to volume as *loud* or *soft*, rather than high or low to avoid confusion with the parameters of pitch).

The specific wave measurement that affects volume is *amplitude*. We have learned that molecules are set into motion by introducing some vibrating body through air. In the resulting sound wave, the distance between the 0 point (where the vibration started) and the maximum "height" of the waveform is the amplitude. In terms of what we hear, the greater the amplitude, the louder the sound. Note that the negative part of the wave also produces sound. It also has amplitude, just in another direction, expressed as a

negative number.

Sound engineers measure volume in dB, short for *decibels*. More specifically, they measure decibels of sound pressure level (dB SPL). It is beyond the scope of this book to fully explain sound pressure and different types of dB. The higher the dB SPL, the louder a sound will seem (fig. 4.46). Since it corresponds so well to the human ear's perception of loudness, dB SPL is what sound engineers generally mean when they say dB.

Varying levels of volume in music, used creatively, are known as dynamics. The difference in dB between the loudest sound and the quietest sound an instrument can make (or in a piece of music or record-

Figure 4.44: As the string is shortened, the guitar plays higher pitches.

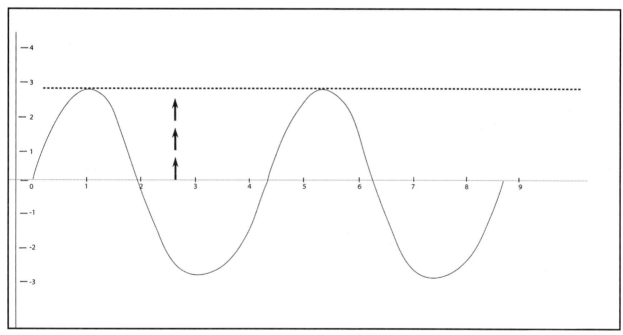

Figure 4.45: Amplitude is the height of the waveform; that is, the distance between the 0 point and the highest peak of the wave.

ing) is called dynamic range. Our ears can detect sounds from 0 dB (the threshold of hearing) to 130 dB (the threshold of pain). This is known as the dynamic range of the ear (fig. 4.47).

Timbre

Timbre is another word for *tone color* or *tone*. It describes how the ear perceives the individual characteristic of a sound. It allows you to differentiate one instrument from another, even if the instruments are

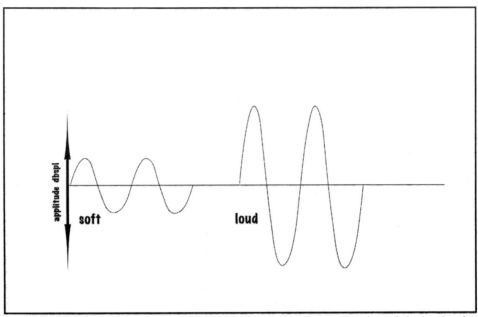

Figure 4.46: The greater the pressure of a sound wave, the greater the amplitude and the louder the volume.

playing the same note at the same volume. Timbre is a quality that is often described in subjective language similar to that of visual arts, as we shall see below.

Up to this point, we have used sine waves to illustrate sound waves because they are simple. However, few sounds produce only one wave; most produce many. Every instrument, when it makes a sound (a vibration in air), creates a *fundamental* frequency (the lowest pitch, and the main one our ears identify) and a series of other, less audible frequencies. All of these vibrations happen at the same time. When we pluck a guitar string, in addition to the main frequency (pitch) we hear, it vibrates at many other higher frequencies with different levels of intensity (dB SPL). These additional, less audible frequencies are called *overtones* or partials, which musicians also refer to as *harmonics*. For our purposes, we will use the term harmonics.

Harmonics occur above the fundamental

pitch in a natural, mathematically measurable series called the overtone series and are an integral part of western music and tuning (fig 4.48). Every sound we hear has its own unique combination of frequencies—its own *harmonic structure*, or the degree to which each harmonic frequency in the sound is audible. Harmonics are what give instruments their characteristic sounds or timbres. An instrument's harmonic structure is affected by its shape, size, the material it is made of, and how it is played.

We might describe a cello playing an A as "very mellow," while a trombone playing the same note may sound "brassy." When discussing the quality of sound from an instrument or particular player, picturesque language is often used. Subjective descriptions may include words like "pure," "crisp," "tinny," or "honking." Commonly used terms include "bright", referring to the audible "presence" of certain high frequencies; "dark", referring to the compar-

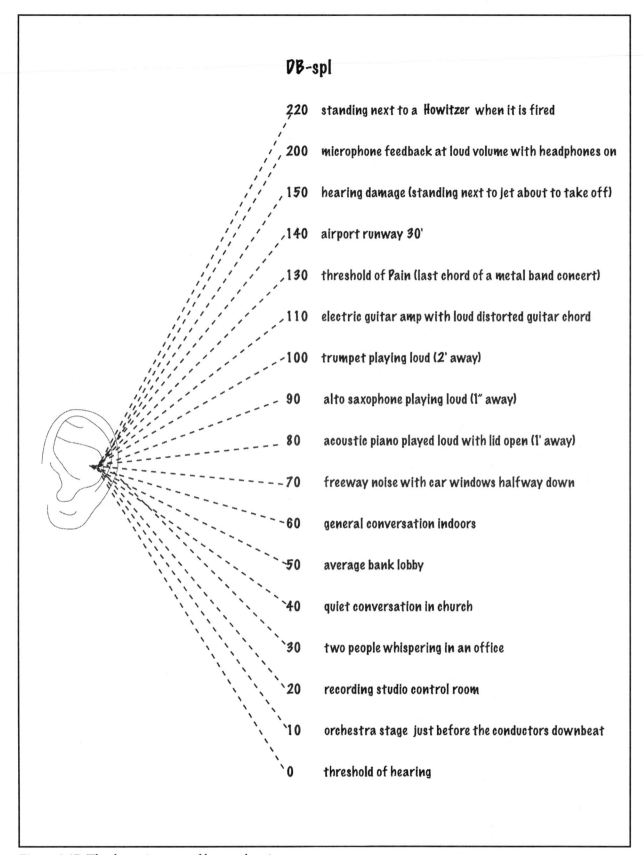

Figure 4.47: The dynamic range of human hearing.

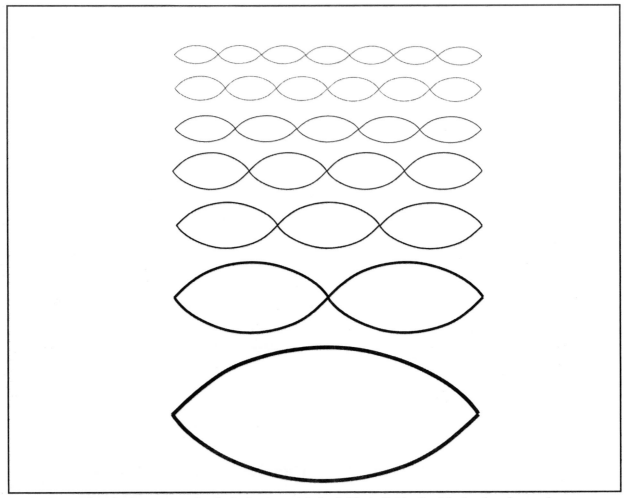

Figure 4.48: What the harmonics of a plucked string might look like individually. The loudest, lowest frequency we hear is the fundamental of the note. Notes above it are harmonics.

ative lack of audible highs; and "muddy", describing a sound that is indistinct, often because of low notes played too close together at the same time.

Phase

Another parameter important to sound frequencies and timbre is phase. Phase refers to the relationship of the timing of different sound waves. When different frequencies of waves vibrate simultaneously, their amplitudes are added together. Remember, all waves have both positive and negative amplitude, so the result of the "addition" is that some audible frequencies increase and others decrease. This of course affects the timbre of an instrument (fig 4.49).

When two waves begin at the same time and travel together to the same peak and negative levels the result is a wave that is twice as loud as the single waves. If two waves begin at the same time but travel to precisely opposite peaks the resulting wave is canceled out (phase cancellation), so playing two signals with exactly opposite waves will produce silence! Of course, most sounds have varying frequencies, creating a less even, complex waveform when added (fig 4.50).

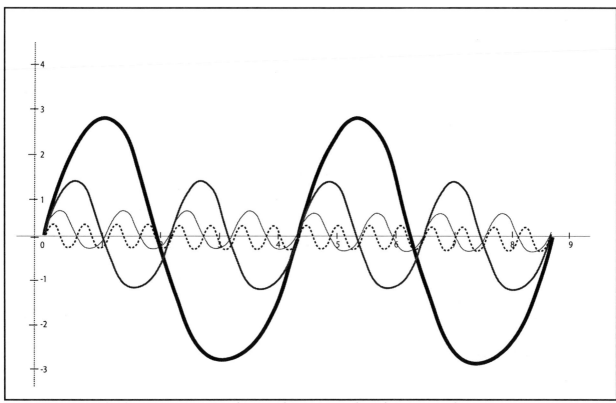

Figure 4.49: Complex harmonic structure of a note showing waveform frequencies' phases. The extent to which various harmonics are heard in a given sound affects that sound's timbre.

Understanding harmonics is directly related to the recording and production of music. Engineers choose certain equipment (i.e., amplifiers, microphones, consoles, and tape machines) for recording a particular instrument because it brings out the best qualities of that instrument. The basis for this choice is often a device's response to particular frequencies. This quality of a device is described as, unsurprisingly, its *frequency response*.

Envelope

Sound engineers and sound designers may describe the characteristic timbre of a sound in terms of its *envelope*. A sound envelope refers to the dynamic gradation of volume over a period of time. There are several parameters of sound in the envelope. The basic ones are *attack*, *decay*, *sustain*, and *release*. *Attack* is how fast a sound starts, specifically, the measurement of time between 0 and peak. *Decay* is how long a sound takes to go from peak to a steady volume. *Sustain* is how long the sound remains at a steady volume. *Release* is how long it takes for the sound to dissipate to silence after the sustain has completed. This set of terms is abbreviated ADSR (fig. 4.51).

Many instruments can play the same note but sound different due to different playing styles and the nature of the resulting notes' envelopes. For example, the G string on a violin when bowed (slow attack), would have a different envelope and sound than the same string when plucked (quick attack). Sound designers (those who work in synthesis) and engineers manipulate these characteristics to "re-shape" sound.

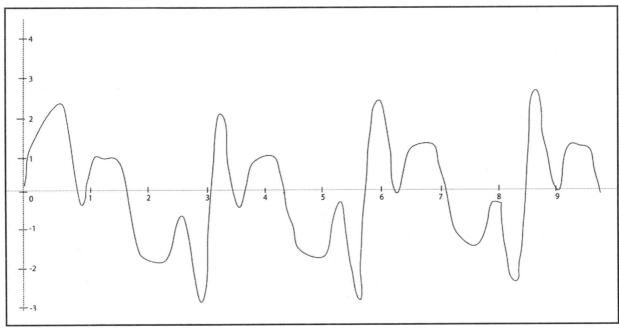

Figure 4.50: What a complex waveform might look like after adding all harmonics' waveforms.

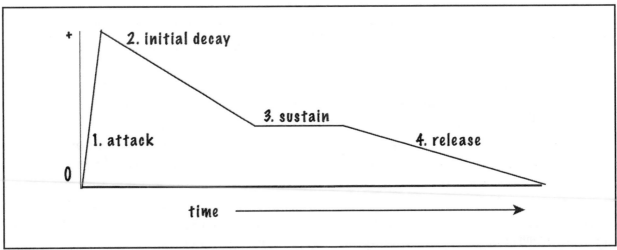

Figure 4.51: The envelope of a piano when a note is struck without the sustain pedal. Attack = time from 0 to peak. Decay = time from peak to steady volume. Sustain = length of steady volume. Release = time from end of sustain to silence.

Lesson 6 Practical Exercises

1. Why is a sound wave not a sound?

2. What is a transducer? What is the organic equivalent in the human ear?

3. What is TTS?

4. What are four parameters of a sound envelope?

5. What does dB-SPL stand for?

6. What is the dynamic range of human hearing (low to high) in dB-SPL?

7. What are the three scientifically measurable parameters of a sound wave?

8. For each of the three parameters, what unit of measurement is used to quantify it?

9. In terms that musicians might use, what are the three properties of a musical note?

10. Which of the three sound wave parameters listed in question 7 correspond(s) to which two note properties listed in question 9?
_____ corresponds to _____
_____ and _____ correspond to _____

11. What is another word for harmonics? What are they?

12. Which of the three note properties is associated with harmonics?

Lesson 7 Pitch Notation

From the previous lesson we know that sound is produced by vibrations acting upon air molecules, creating waves that the ear interprets as sound. Sounds can be identified as either musical tones or noise. When the frequency of vibration is regular, the ear will perceive a *pitch*, which is a musical tone or *note*. Each note has its own specific frequency of vibration (cycles per second), which our ears perceive as pitch. An established system of musical symbols is used to communicate pitch. These include the staff, clefs, notes, and accidentals. Seen all at once, it can be intimidating (fig. 4.52).

We looked at a staff briefly in chapter 2. Pitch notation takes place on the five lines and four spaces of a staff. Each line and each space identifies a specific pitch (frequency of vibration); a note's position on the staff determines its pitch. The lines and spaces, numbered from bottom to top, also have letter names (fig. 4.53).

Clefs

Five lines and four spaces are only adequate to represent nine pitches. In contrast, the piano has 88 keys, with each key representing a different pitch. To determine which range of pitches are represented by a particular staff, we use a *clef*. A clef is a symbol representing one of the seven letters of the musical alphabet. When placed on a staff, it assigns a

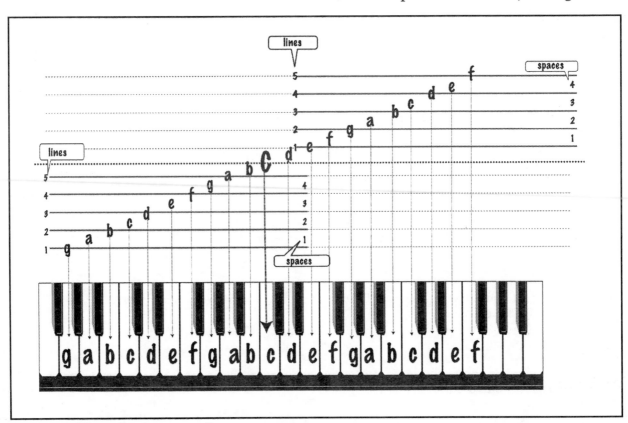

Figure 4.52: The staff and corresponding notes on a piano.

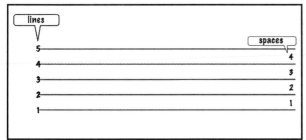

Figure 4.53: The five lines and four spaces of the staff. Staff lines and spaces are counted from the bottom up.

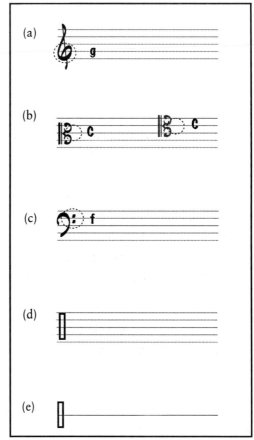

Figure 4.54 a. Treble clef (G clef).
b. Alto and Tenor clefs, noted with the movable C clef.
c. Bass clef (F clef) is for the low register.
d. Percussion clef.
e. Percussion clef.

definite pitch to each line and space. There are three standard clefs used in pitch notation. From highest to lowest they are the G clef, the C clef and the F clef. There is also a percussion clef for non-pitched instruments.

The G clef 𝄞 is more commonly called the *treble clef* and assigns G to the second staff line by stylishly circling the G line (fig. 4.54a). This clef establishes the staff with the highest range of notes. When counting lines and spaces on the staff, count from bottom up.

The C clef 𝄡 is a moveable clef. The vertex of the C clef identifies middle C (fig. 4.54b). It is called the *alto clef* or the *tenor clef,* depending on its position on the staff lines. These clefs notate middle ranges. The alto clef is more common. It indicates that the middle line of the staff is middle C.

The F clef 𝄢 is commonly called the *bass clef*; the two dots straddle the fourth line, indicating F below Middle C (fig 4.54c). The bass clef is used to notate the lowest range of notes.

The percussion clef is written either ‖ or ‖ (figs 4.54 d & e). The various drums or percussion indicated by a percussion clef vary. To be certain of clarity, an arranger will write which drum is notated on which line or space.

For pitched instruments, a clef placed at the beginning of a staff tells the musician which notes are represented by the lines and spaces in that staff. Study the lines and spaces of each clef until you have them memorized. Some beginning musicians practice the line and space names separately, for example, "EGBDF" for the lines of the treble clef.

For percussion staves, the line or lines can represent what the arranger wants in a given place. Figure 4.56 shows two typical uses of percussion clefs and staves.

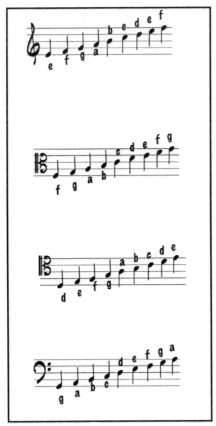

Figure 4.55: Note names for clefs and staves that represent specific pitches.

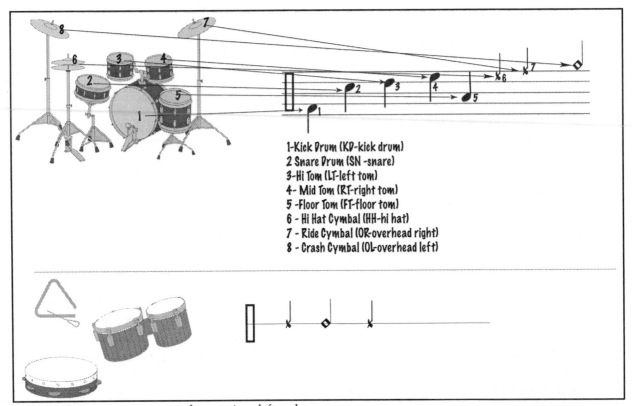

1-Kick Drum (KD-kick drum)
2 Snare Drum (SN -snare)
3-Hi Tom (LT-left tom)
4- Mid Tom (RT-right tom)
5 -Floor Tom (FT-floor tom)
6 - Hi Hat Cymbal (HH-hi hat)
7 - Ride Cymbal (OR-overhead right)
8 - Crash Cymbal (OL-overhead left)

Figure 4.56: Two common uses of percussion clefs and staves.

Grand Staff and Ledger Lines

The range of a musical instrument-how high and low it can play-determines which clef is used to notate its music. Some instruments, such as harp or piano, have such wide ranges that their music requires two staves (plural of staff) at once. For these instruments, and for 4-part choral music, a grand staff, sometimes called the great staff is used. The *grand staff* uses both a treble clef staff and a bass clef staff which are connected by a vertical line, often accompanied by a bracket (fig. 4.57).

Figure 4.57: The Grand Staff.

Even with a grand staff, not all of the notes used in music are within the two staves. The lines and spaces continue above and below the staff but are not drawn until they are needed for high or low notes. When a note falls outside the range of the staff, a short line is drawn through, above or below the note (if it falls on a line or a space, respectively). These short lines are called *ledger lines* (figs. 4.58 a and b); they are "extended" staff lines, invisible until needed.

Notes on the Piano

The staff and the clefs provide the basis for representing pitches. Each line and each space represents a specific pitch. When notes are placed on the staff, they inform the performer which pitches to execute. We give these pitches letter names. Looking at the white keys on a piano (fig. 4.59), their names are A, B, C, D, E, F, and G. Notice that the pattern of the keys repeats. After G, you return to A again, and the position of the second A is the same in relation to the piano keys' pattern as the first.

Study the picture and take some time to

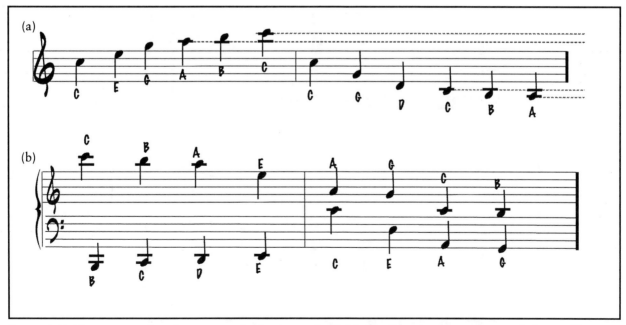

Figure 4.58: To notate pitches that are outside the range of a clef, ledger lines are drawn above or below staff, as needed, for notes beyond the staff's regular range. a. Treble clef's ledger lines. b. Grand Staff's ledger lines.

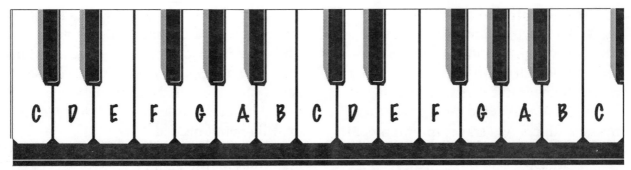

Figure 4.59: Notes on the piano.

become familiar with where each note's letter name falls in the black-and-white pattern of the keys. D is probably the easiest to find at first. If you put your right index finger on D, your thumb easily falls onto C. Find all of the Ds, Cs, and As on a keyboard, then learn to identify other notes.

The notes of the piano correspond to the lines and spaces on the staves (go back to fig. 4.52, the large keyboard and staff, as a reference). Musicians the world over use

and understand this system. Notice that so far we have only given letter names to the white keys. All black keys have two possible names. The black key immediately next to a white key is a half step away from it in pitch. These keys can be named for the white keys near them: the black key just above D is called D sharp. However, the same key is also a half step below E, and can also be called E flat (fig. 4.60 a & b).

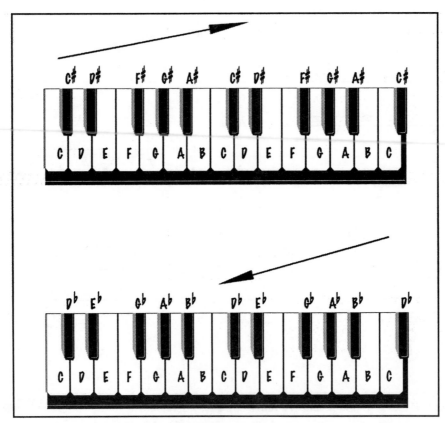

Figure 4.60: Naming the black keys. a: sharps; b: flats.

Accidentals

In order to notate these "in between" pitches, we use symbols called *accidentals*. Accidentals next to a note on the staff (immediately to the left of the note) tell the performer to play these "in between" notes. The *sharp* symbol (♯) is used to indicate a note a half step (fig. 4.61a) above the regular note at that line or space. The *flat* symbol (♭) is used to indicate a note a half step lower than the usual note at a line or space (figure 4.61b). A *natural* (♮) returns the note back to its original pitch after it is altered (fig. 4.61c) All accidentals apply to a note until the end of the measure, unless cancelled by another accidental applied to the same note in that measure.

So how do you know whether to call a black key a flat or sharp? It varies according to context, but the general rule is, when notes are ascending (going up), a note is given its sharp name. When descending (going down), a note is given its flat name (figs. 4.62 and 4.63).

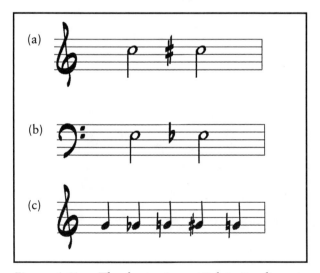

Figures 4.61: a: The sharp raises a pitch to its adjacent key above. b: The flat lowers a pitch to its adjacent key below. c: The natural returns a pitch (from flat or sharp) to its original pitch.

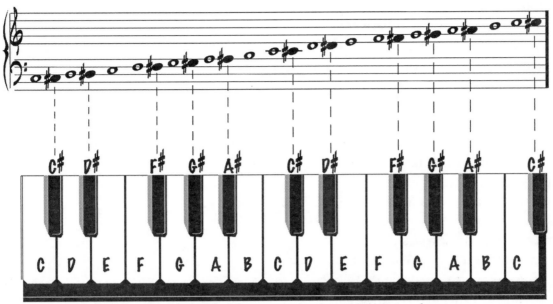

Figure 4.62: *When pitches ascend, the black keys are most often written using sharps.*

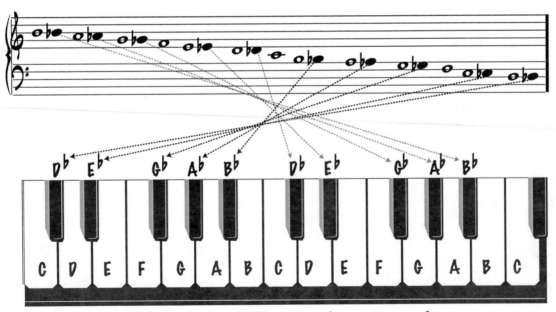

Figure 4.63: *When pitches descend, the black keys are most often written using flats.*

Lesson 7 Practical Exercises

A. Questions

1. It is important to put a clef at the beginning of a staff. Why?

2. What are ledger lines and how are they used?

3. What are the four common clefs used in music?

4. Which clef is movable?

5. What is the name of the symbol used to raise a pitch to the next adjacent note?

6. Name the three accidentals explained in the lesson. Draw each one. Explain the use of each.

B. Visual practice

7. Using quarter notes, notate and label the lines and spaces in treble clef, bass clef and alto clef.

8. Write in the following pitches on the staff. Do not use ledger lines:

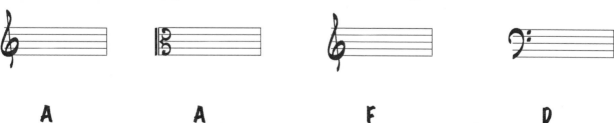

A   A   F   D

9. Identify the following pitches on the piano keyboard:

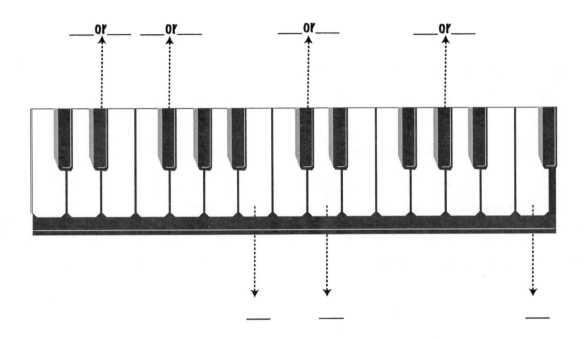

10. Identify the following pitches:

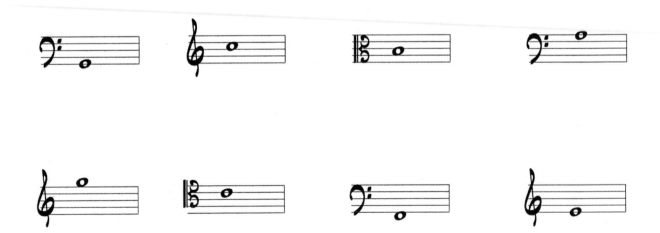

Chapter 5: Melody and Harmony

What you should know:
• What a melody is and how it is supported by harmony
• How to recognize major key signatures, intervals, and chord symbols
• How to transpose a piece of music

Why you should know it:
Most songs have both melody and harmony. Understanding what they are and how to notate them will help you develop a vocabulary consistent with that of musicians and those who support them.

Lesson 8: Melody

Pitches are related to one another in two ways: harmonically and melodically. When notes are played sequentially (one after the other), they are said to have a *melodic* relationship (fig. 5.64). Notes that are sounded simultaneously (at the same time) have a *harmonic* relationship (fig. 5.65). Some musicians describe melody as "horizontal" and harmony as "vertical." I want to emphasize that the ability to

hear and recognize melodic or harmonic relationships requires a long study in ear training and theory; this book and the CD that comes with it do not purport to provide that study. The goal here is simply to ensure that you understand the basic concepts of melody and harmony in order to improve your work as a producer, engineer, or artist, and perhaps open the door to further study.

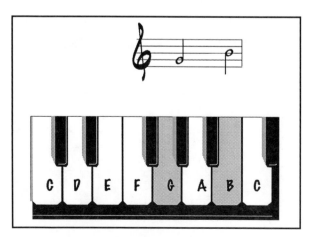

Figure 5.64: A melodic interval.

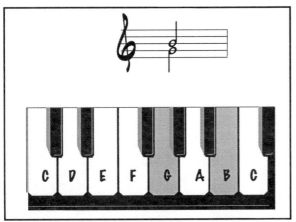

Figure 5.65: A harmonic interval.

Track 25: Two notes played (a) melodically, then (b) harmonically.

Melody can be defined as an organized sequence of single notes. It is the part the lead singer sings or that the solo instrumentalist plays. Melodies are based on relationships between notes and are made of consecutive intervals. An *interval* is the distance between two pitches.

Intervals: Part I

The smallest interval in western music is the *semi-tone*, or *half step*. Any two adjacent notes on a piano are a half step apart (fig 5.66). Play all black and white piano keys in order, ascending and descending, or play each note on one guitar string ascending and descending the frets to hear all the half steps (incidentally, what you have just played is called a *chromatic scale*).

Two half steps equal a *whole step*. Any two notes (black or white) with only one note between them are a whole step apart (fig. 5.67). Starting with these two small intervals, we will discuss scales. More intervals will be covered later in this chapter.

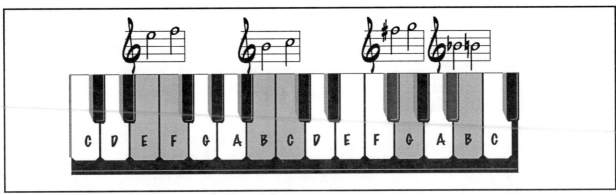

Figure 5.66: Intervals of half steps are always on adjacent notes.

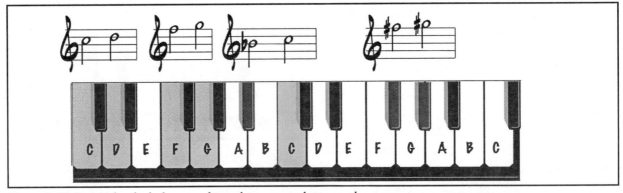

Figure 5.67: Intervals of whole steps always have a note between them.

The major scale

A *scale* is a series of consecutive ascending or descending steps within an *octave* (an 8-note range), with whole steps and half steps in a particular order. There are many scales used in music, but by far the most common is the *major scale*. For the purposes of this book, we will look at the major scale and only touch briefly on another scale called the minor scale.

Track 26: Major scale ascending & descending.

> You can probably already sing a major scale. Sing "Joy to the World." The first eight notes of this Christmas song are a descending major scale. The ascending scale is no doubt familiar too.

Track 27: "Joy to the World" (a descending major scale).

It is easy to play a C major scale on the piano: start at C and play each white note until you reach the next C. The white keys — all of the unaltered letter-named notes (C D E F G A B) — are *diatonic* to the key of C. This means that these and no other notes make up a C major scale (fig. 5.68).

Conversely, a note outside the scale is *non-diatonic*, also called *chromatic*. For C major, it is easy to know which notes are non-diatonic: all black keys are chromatic to C. Chromatic notes for other major scales are not so obvious without learning major scales thoroughly. Notice that the first note of the scale, also known as the *keynote* or *tonic*, is the same as the last. As you might guess, it is also the "name" of the scale. The keynote of C major is C; the keynote of A major is A, etc.

Starting with the keynote, examine the steps between each note of the C scale. The distance between sequential letter-named notes is either a whole or a half step. From middle C up to the next white key, D, is a whole step, also called a *major second* (abbreviated *Maj. 2*). From D to E is also a whole step, because there is a black key in between the two keys. However, there is no black key between the E and the F; therefore from E to F is a half step, also called a *minor second* (abbreviated *min. 2*).

A major scale is **always** in that specific

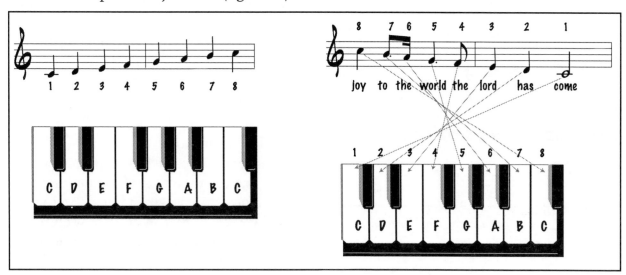

Figure 5.68: Notes in a C major scale ascending and descending.

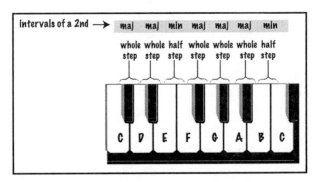

Figure 5.69: The intervallic relationship of a C major scale.

pattern of steps, ascending, starting from the keynote: WHOLE, WHOLE, half, WHOLE, WHOLE, WHOLE, half. If we maintain the intervallic pattern, we can formulate a major scale pattern starting from any note.

As your ears will quickly tell you listening to Track 28, if we start the scale pattern on the note D, we cannot maintain the intervallic relationships needed for a major scale on just the white keys. We get WHOLE, half, WHOLE, WHOLE, WHOLE, half, WHOLE (fig. 5.70).

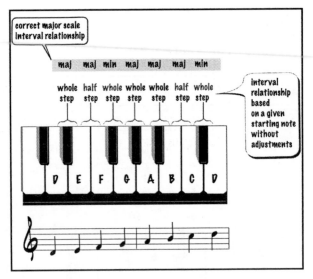

Figure 5.70: 8 consecutive notes, white keys only, beginning on D.

⬤ Track 28: Figure 5.70, as written: 8 steps up from D on just white keys

Black keys are needed to play the right notes to complete the major scale. As explained in lesson 7, we name and notate these pitches using accidentals. Using the major scale pattern of whole and half steps, figure out which notes (from the black keys) are needed to create a D major scale.

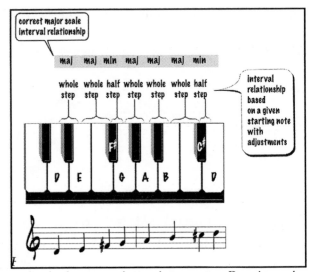

maintain the correct intervals to create a D major scale.

⬤ Track 29: D major scale

The derivation of a few more major scales may be seen in figures 5.72 a -d. Notice that each requires a different set of black keys (accidentals) to create a major scale. Notice that once you make one adjustment to an interval (using a black key), you must then measure the next interval from the new note.

The minor scale

The minor scale has a different intervallic pattern than that of the major scale. The minor scale is, ascending from the keynote, WHOLE, half, WHOLE, WHOLE, half, WHOLE, WHOLE. The minor scale is considered sad or melancholic. This feeling comes from the sound of the minor

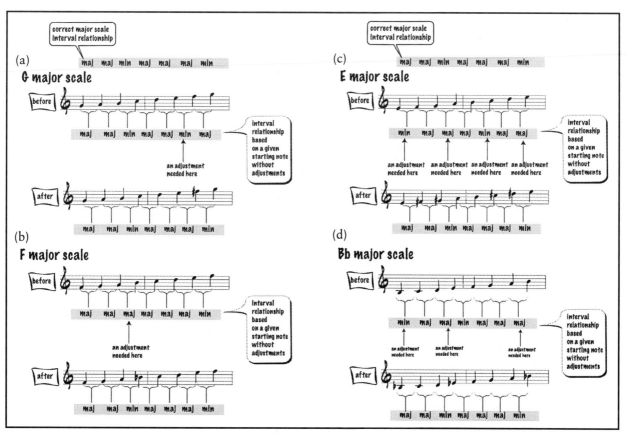

Figures 5.72 a –d: Using the same major scale pattern of whole and half steps (major & minor 2nds), we can determine the notes needed for a major scale starting on any note.

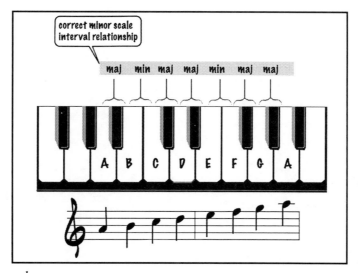

Figure 5.73: The A minor scale.

Track 30: An A minor scale.

second (half step) between the second and third notes of the scale (fig. 5.73). Correct intervallic relationships for a minor scale are W, h, W, W h, W, W.

If we compare a major scale to its parallel minor scale, we see which notes must be lowered to change a major into a minor scale (figs. 5.74 a & b). Remember that

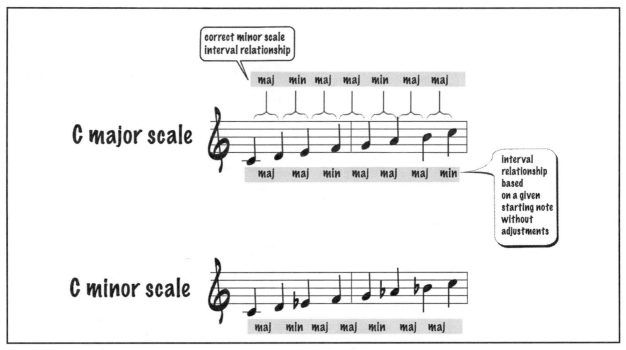

Figure 5.74 a & b: Compare the C major scale to the C minor scale. Lowering the 3rd, 6th, and 7th notes of a major scale changes the intervallic relationship of the notes to those of a minor scale.

Track 31: (a) C major scale; (b) C minor scale

when one note is altered, if affects the scale interval both above and below it.

Intervals: Part II

As stated above, intervals are based on the distance between notes. We identify an interval between two notes by counting the steps between the starting pitch and the ending pitch. The resulting count is the interval's name. We will concern ourselves only with intervals within a major scale (fig 5.75).

Remember, the musical alphabet is just seven letters long. The "end" (8th) note of a scale is really just the first note again. The distance from one letter-named note to the next note with the <u>same</u> letter name (higher or lower) is an octave (fig 5.76), commonly abbreviated *8ve*. An interval of octave is eight steps, as you can see from

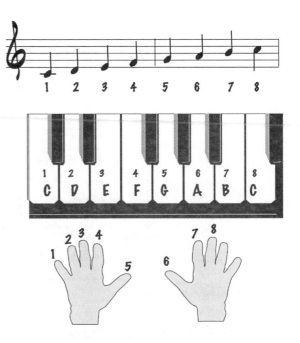

Figure 5.75: Identify intervals by counting the number of fingers from the starting pitch to the ending pitch. The result is the interval's name.

78

your finger count. *Primary* intervals are smaller than an octave.

Returning to our C major scale, we will use our fingers to count up the intervals between each scale degree and the first note of the scale, or count up the lines and spaces between them on a staff (fig 5.76). If we number the scale degrees after the first note—D is the 2nd scale degree, E is the 3rd, etc.—it happens that these numbers are the names of the intervals that are created between the keynote (C) and each other note traveling up the scale (fig 5.76).

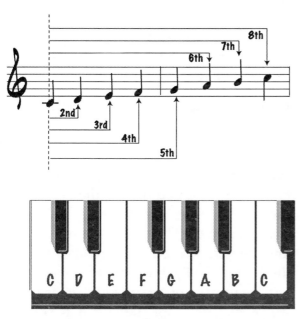

Figure 5.76: All the intervals between the root and other notes in a major scale.

Interval qualities

In addition to intervals formed between each scale degree and the keynote (as described above), intervals are also formed between each scale degree and each other scale degree. Each of the resulting intervals has a different sound or "flavor" which musicians call the *quality* of the interval. There are five interval qualities: perfect,

major, minor, diminished, and augmented. These descriptive names follow a particular pattern:

The fundamental intervals in music are the first three intervals in the harmonic series (discussed in chapter 4). They are the octave, the fifth, and the fourth (8ve, 5th, 4th). Because of this naturally-occurring relationship and their pure-sounding quality, exact intervals of an octave, fifth, or fourth are called *perfect* intervals Seconds, thirds, sixths, or sevenths (2nds, 3rds, 6ths, or 7ths) are never called "perfect," but are primarily *major* or *minor*.

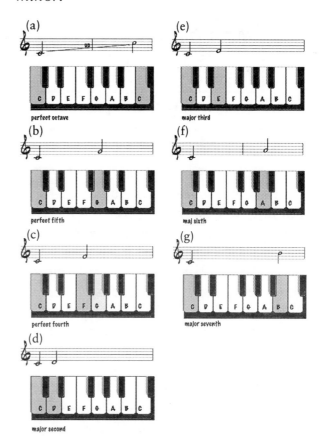

Figures 5.77 a – g: A major scale's intervals and interval qualities on the staff and keyboard.

Let us examine the whole intervals possible in a major scale. With time and study of an instrument, musicians simply "know" intervals and their qualities, much

Interval name	Abbreviation	# of half steps	# of whole + half steps
Minor 2nd	min. 2	= half step	
Major 2nd	Maj. 2	= 2 half steps	= whole step (or just "step")
Minor 3rd	Min. 3	= 3 half steps	= 1 step + 1 half step
Major 3rd	Maj. 3	= 4 half steps	= 2 whole steps
Perfect 4th	p4	= 5 half steps	= 2 steps + 1 half step
Perfect 5th	p5	= 7 half steps	= 3 steps + 1 half step
Minor 6th	min. 6	= 8 half steps	= 4 whole steps
Major 6th	Maj. 6	= 9 half steps	= 4 steps + 1 half step
Minor 7th	min. 7	= 10 half steps	= 5 whole steps
Major 7th	Maj. 7	= 11 half steps	= 5 steps + 1 half step
Perfect Octave	p8ve	= 12 half steps	= 6 whole steps

Figure 5.78: Interval sizes.

like we "know" multiplication tables. At one time we had to add up three 4's, but now we just remember 3 x 4 = 12. While studying, you can calculate interval qualities by "adding up" (counting) whole and half steps between two notes. (Note: some people prefer to add larger intervals. For example, Major 6th = P5 + Major 2. As long as your method is accurate, do what is easiest for you to memorize.)

Altered Intervals

Slightly increasing or decreasing an interval's size changes its "flavor" significantly (fig. 5.79). An interval a half step smaller than minor or perfect is described as *diminished*. If it is a half step larger than major or perfect it described as *augmented*.

Thus, our interval size chart grows. Notice that intervals sometimes are the same size (the same number of half steps), but have different names. The name is based on how they are written and how they function harmonically. Intervals of equal size that are written differently are *enharmonic equivalents*, or simply described as *enharmonic* to one another.

Keys and Key Signatures

Melody and harmony combine to establish a sense of *key*, or *tonality*. Tonality can be described as the sense of a particular note being the "resting place" or "home" of a piece of music. This note is the first note in the scale, and is sometimes called the *tonic* or *key note* or *tone center*. In many melodies, it is the last note of the song. So in the key of G, when reaching

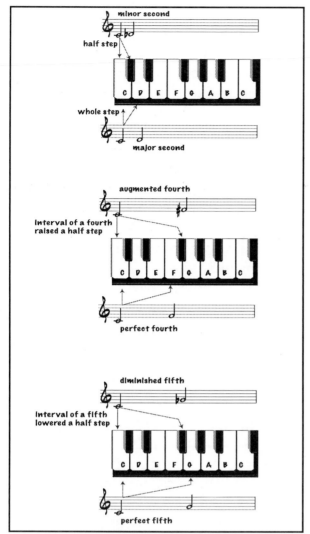

Figures 5.79 a – c: Altered intervals. Specifically, a minor 2nd, augmented 4th, and diminished 5th.

the melodic note G and a G chord (see glossary) at the end, the listener is left with a sense of the song being finished.

Interval name	Abbreviation	#of half steps	# of whole or enharmonic
Augmented 2nd	Aug. 2 (or +2)	= 3 half steps	(same as min. 3)
Diminished 3rd	dim. 3 (or °3)	= 2 half steps	(same as Maj. 2)
Augmented 4th also called a "tritone"	Aug. 4 (or +4)	= 6 half steps	= 3 whole steps
Diminished 5th also called a "tritone"	dim. 5 (or °5)	= 6 half steps	= 3 whole steps
Augmented 6th	Aug. 6 (or +6)	= 10 half steps	(same as min. 7)
Diminished 7th	dim. 7 (or °7)	= 9 half steps	(same as Maj. 6)

Figure 5.80: Altered interval sizes.

Tonality is probably something that your ears already understand. Again, sing "Joy to the World," but stop at the 2nd to last note. Do you feel how your ear wants to hear the last note in order to find a "place to rest?" The last note is the tonic.

If we write a melody in the key of E major (i.e., using the E major scale), to maintain the E tonality ("E feels like home") we will need F#, G#, C# and D# (refer back to fig. 5.72c). It would be cumbersome to place accidentals every time one of these notes is needed in the music. To make the music easier to read, a *key signature* is placed at the beginning of the music.

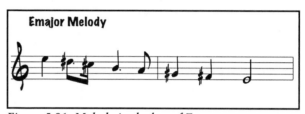

Figure 5.81: Melody in the key of E.

Key signature is something like a "You Are Here" sign on a map; it helps a musician identify the tonality of the music before beginning to play. It is written as a specific set of sharps and flats immediately after the clef sign, but before the time signature (fig. 5.82). It tells the performer to play a certain set of sharps or flats to a note throughout the entire piece of music (fig. 5.83).

E major Key Signature

Figure 5.82: A key signature is placed directly after the clef and before the time signature.

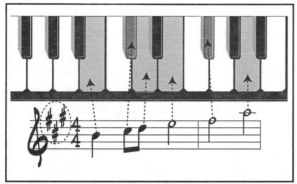

Figure 5.83: If a player sees the key signature noted, then reads the pitches that follow in 5.83a, he will play the shaded notes in 5.83b.

The sharps or flats of a key signature are always placed on the staff in the order indicated in figures 5.84 & 5.85. The sharped or flatted notes are always in effect unless canceled by an accidental in the piece. An accidental in a given measure stays in effect for a pitch only to the end of that measure. (Exception: If effecting a note tied to a note in the next measure, the accidental remains in effect for the duration of the 2nd measure).

Figures 5.84: The correct order of sharps in key signatures on treble and bass clefs.

Figures 5.85: The correct order of flats in key signatures on treble and bass clefs.

Go back to figures 5.72 a – d (earlier in this chapter). The "before" pictures are sets of 8 notes, in order, that did not have the proper intervals to be a major scale. We had to alter certain pitches to create the correct intervals. The altered pitches are the same ones that make up the key signature for a given key. Based on those alterations, we can derive the key signatures for those keys: G has one sharp; F has one flat; E has 4 sharps, etc.

Each major key shares its key signature with one minor key (its *relative minor*) and with other tonalities known as *modes*. This is why it says above that a key signature "helps" determine the actual key (chords, melody, and the "feeling of home"). We have concerned ourselves with major key signatures only. Delve further into other keys and modes with a good music theory book.

The *Circle of Fifths* (figure 5.86) is a system to help musicians memorize key signatures. Since all key signatures have different numbers of sharps and flats, but the sharps (or flats) are in the same order, we can arrange a circle of keys in the order of the added sharps (or subtracted flats).

If we start at the top of this circle at C major we see there are no required sharps or flats and therefore no annotated key signature. As we move to the right to G major (a fifth higher), we see that we must add one sharp to the key signature. If we move to the left to F major (a fifth lower), we see that we must add one flat to the key signature. By using this process of adding flats (or removing sharps) while moving **left,** or adding sharps (or removing flats) while moving **right,** we can go around the circle and see the relationships of sharps and flats to each key. You should memorize all key signatures utilizing the circle of fifths.

Transposition

So if C is so nice and easy, why doesn't everyone always play in C? Why bother with D or harder-to-learn keys like Ab? Every human voice and every instrument has limits as to how high and low it can sound. The *range* of a singer (or instrument) is all the notes that singer (or instrument) can hit. When we write music we need to consider the range(s) of the instrument(s) that will be performing it, especially of the lead singer or instrument.

Any melody can be played on the piano, as it has such a wide range, but voice or instrument ranges may make it difficult or impossible for a particular musician to perform a particular melody in the original key. A man with a low bass voice will not be able to sing the same melody in the same key that a woman with a high soprano range can sing.

The choice of key is an important one. When recording a song, even if it is possible for a singer to hit the notes of a melody in a particular key, it may not be with his or her best sound. A different key may bring out the singer's best tone quality and significantly improve the

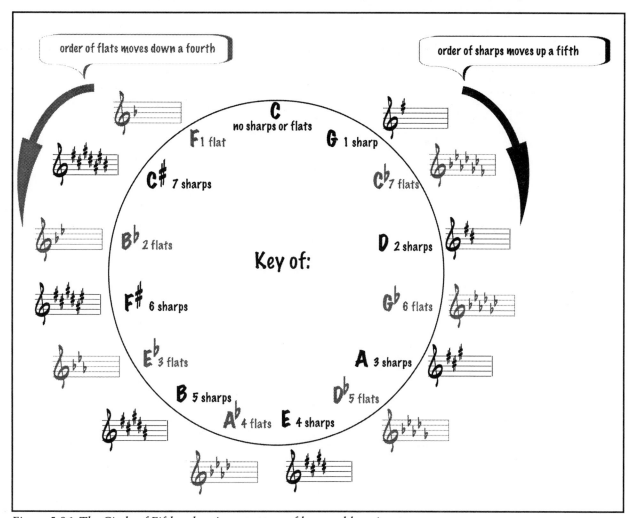

Figure 5.86: The Circle of Fifths, showing a pattern of keys and key signatures.

sound — and marketability — of the song. The important point is that we want the same melody (the same intervallic relationships between notes) but need it to be within the range of the singer. To do this, we change the key. To *transpose* music is to write it in a key other than the one in which it was originally written. Transposition takes the original pitches and moves them proportionately, relative to their positions in the original melody. There are many ways to transpose. The process we will use is called *scale degree transposition*.

In scale degree transposition, we must first identify the key of the original

melody, then the *scale degree* of each note of the melody. We touched on scale degrees when learning about intervals. To determine the scale degrees of a given key, write out and label each note in an ascending major scale, starting with the keynote as scale degree 1.

In figure 5.87 a-e you can see a melody in the key of C. You then see all the steps it take to transpose it to the key of D, using scale degrees as a guide. Each step is explained in detail on the next page. Knowing the scale degrees of a melody, we can easily transpose it to another key, keeping the scale degree relationship relative (fig. 5.87b).

Figure 5.87 a - e: By keeping the same scale degrees of the melody, we can transpose the melody from the key of C to the key of D.

The transposition process:

1. Examine the original melody, as written. Note its key signature.

2. Write out the scale for the original key signature.

3. Label the scale degrees of the scale.

4. Returning to the original melody, label each note of the melody with its scale degree.

5. Write out the scale of the new key and label its scale degrees.

6. Referring to the scale degrees of the original melody, carefully re-write the melody with the correct scale degrees of the new key.

Transpose a simple melody with this step-by-step procedure. Try transposing the melody below, following the steps as explained. Important: when transposing melodies, transpose notes either all up or all down. For this exercise, transpose up.

Original Melody

1. Identify the key signature of the original melody (refer to the Circle of 5ths if necessary). Using its key signature, write out the original key's major scale on the staff below.

2. Label the scale degrees for reference.

3. Identify and label each scale degree of the original melody. The melody for this music begins on the sixth degree of the scale.

4. Identify the key signature of the new key. We want this melody to be in A major. Write out the major scale of the new key below and label the scale degrees for reference.

5. Based on the scale degrees identified in the original key, re-write the notes, using original rhythms, in the correct lines or spaces for the corresponding scale degrees in the new key.

You have now transposed a song from E major to A major, up a fourth. Check your work with figures 5.88 a - f.

Figure 5.88: Step-by-step transposition, correctly completed.

Lesson 8 Exercises

A. Questions

1. How is an interval measured?

2. What is the difference between a harmonic interval and a melodic interval?

3. What is the smallest interval?

4. Which intervals' qualities are perfect?

5. Which intervals' qualities are either major or minor?

6. What is a key signature and what does it tell the musician?

7. What note is scale degree six in the key of A major?

8. What note is scale degree four in the key of B flat major?

9. What is the quality of the resulting interval when you lower a perfect interval by a half step?

10. What is the quality of the resulting interval when you lower a major interval by a half step?

11. What is the quality of the resulting interval when you raise a perfect or major interval by a half step?

12. Which three scale degrees are lowered to alter a scale from major to minor?

Lesson 8 Exercises

B. Visual Practice - 1

Major Scales
Notate a major scale starting on the first note of each staff below by adding accidentals to make the correct pattern of half-steps and whole-steps.

Lesson 8 Exercises

B. Visual Practice - 2

Identify Keyboard Intervals
Identify and label the following intervals:

1. _____

2. _____

3. _____

4. _____

5. _____

6. _____

7. _____

8. _____

9. _____

10. _____

11. _____

12. _____

13. _____

14. _____

15. _____

16. _____

Lesson 8 Exercises

B. Visual Practice - 3

Notate Intervals

Based on the starting note, create the correct intervals by adding the correct note before or after (as indicated by the empty space on either the left or right of the given note).

1. major 7th
2. minor 7th
3. minor 3rd
4. diminished 4th

5. minor 3rd
6. perfect 4th
7. minor 6th
8. perfect 4th

9. major 3rd
10. major 3rd
11. major 6th
12. major 3rd

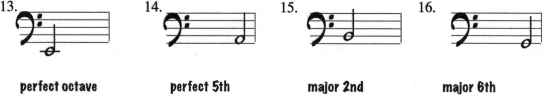

13. perfect octave
14. perfect 5th
15. major 2nd
16. major 6th

Lesson 8 Exercises

B. Visual Practice - 4

Identify key signatures
Write in the name of the correct key for each key signature written below.

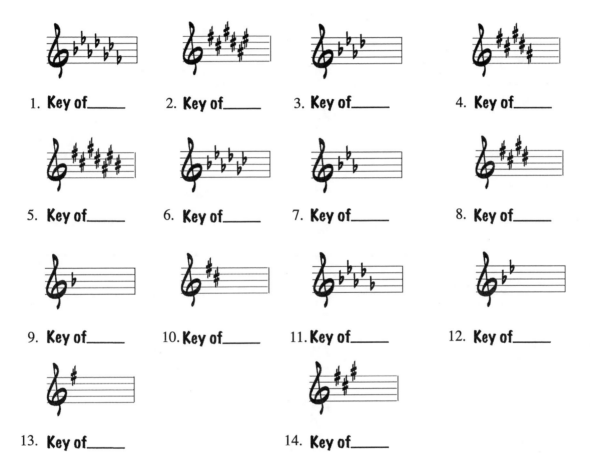

1. Key of_____

2. Key of_____

3. Key of_____

4. Key of_____

5. Key of_____

6. Key of_____

7. Key of_____

8. Key of_____

9. Key of_____

10. Key of_____

11. Key of_____

12. Key of_____

13. Key of_____

14. Key of_____

Lesson 8 Exercises

B. Visual Practice - 5

Notate Key Signatures
Write in the following major key signatures:

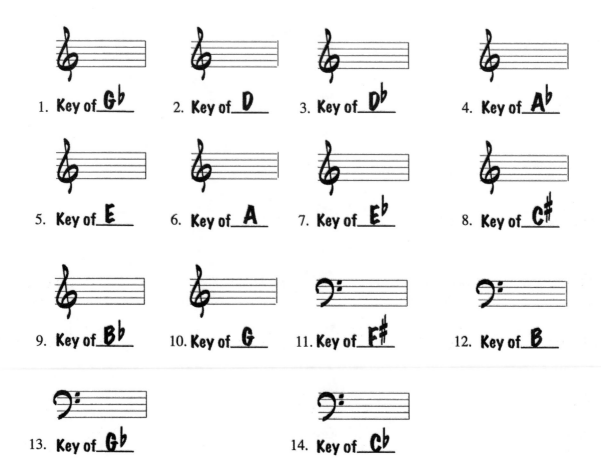

1. Key of G♭

2. Key of D

3. Key of D♭

4. Key of A♭

5. Key of E

6. Key of A

7. Key of E♭

8. Key of C♯

9. Key of B♭

10. Key of G

11. Key of F♯

12. Key of B

13. Key of G♭

14. Key of C♭

Lesson 8 Exercises

B. Visual Practice - 6

Identify Written Intervals
Identify and label the following intervals and their qualities, e.g., "Aug 4th," or "min. 7th."

1. Interval of a _____

2. Interval of a _____

3. Interval of a _____

4. Interval of a _____

5. Interval of a _____

6. Interval of a _____

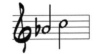

7. Interval of a _____

8. Interval of a _____

9. Interval of a _____

10. Interval of a _____

11. Interval of a _____

12. Interval of a _____

13. Interval of a _____

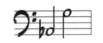

14. Interval of a _____

15. Interval of a _____

16. Interval of a _____

Lesson 8 Exercises   B. Visual Practice - 7

Label the scale degree of each note in the melody below, according to the key signature. Repetition is good exercise to set the information in your mind, so make sure to label every note, except those that are tied.

Key of A, The Song

Lesson 8 Exercises   B. Visual Practice - 8

In the blank staves below, follow the process for transcription: write out the scale of
the original key, and of the new key (G), then transpose the melody "Key of A, the Song" down a
step into "Key of G, The Song".

Key of G, The Song

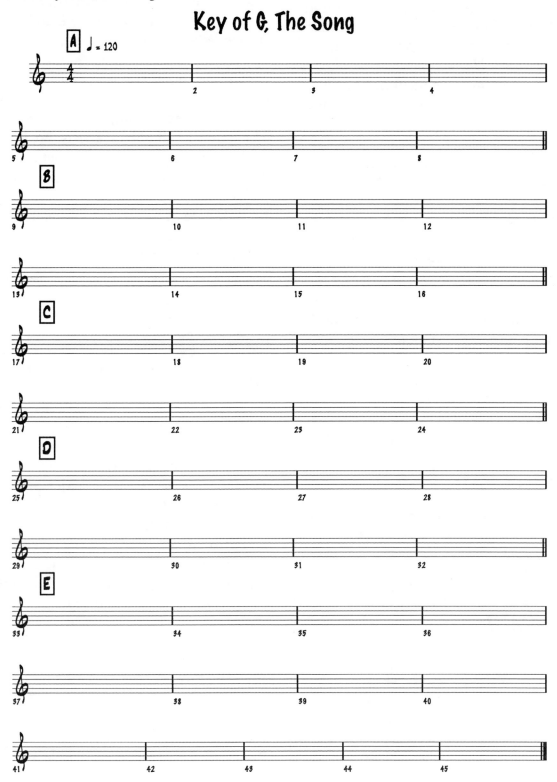

Lesson 9: Harmony and Chords

Notes played in addition to and as support for the melody can be considered *harmony*. When a background singer sings a note above or below the lead singer, we may say he or she is singing a *harmony part*. *Harmony* is also the chords played to accompany a melody. Chords create much of the mood or "background" of a song.

The *harmonic progression* (series of chords) is the setting that will "shade" how the melody sounds. Changing the chords (even slightly) will in fact change the color and mood of the song. Many producers and composers will play with different harmonies to find the right combination for a given melody. In jazz, *re-harmonization* (changing the chords originally written) of standard songs is commonly practiced and is an art itself. Again, musicians study harmony for years. The information given below just gives the briefest overview of chords. The purpose is to make you generally aware of these terms if you hear them, not to give a thorough study in harmony.

Chords are generally built from intervals, as will be seen below. The simplest chords

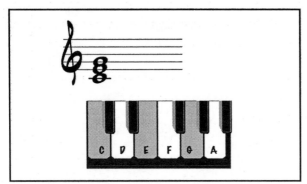

Figure 5.89: Triad as played on the piano and notated on the staff.

are *triads*, three notes played at once. Harmonically simple music, including much popular music, is said to be *triadic*, that is, using only triads in its harmony. There are five qualities of triads: *major*, *minor*, *augmented*, *diminished*, and *suspended/sustained* (or "sus").

Major and minor triads are by far the most common; we will restrict ourselves primarily to explaining these two only. The notes (in all but sus triads) are known as the *root*, *3rd*, and *5th* of the chord. The 3rd and 5th are identified by their intervallic relationship to the root, or the bottom note of the chord. For example, the notes of an A major triad are A (root), C♯ (3rd), and E (5th).

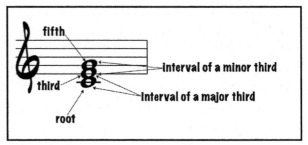

Figure 5.90: Notes of major and minor triads are called root, 3rd, and 5th.

Each triad is built of two intervals of a third. *Major triads* have a major 3rd on the bottom (between root and 3rd) and a minor 3rd on the top (between the 3rd and 5th). *Minor triads* are the reverse: they have a minor 3rd on the bottom (between the root and 3rd) and a major 3rd on the top (between the 3rd and 5th).

Richer, more complicated chords are "built" on triads. Intervals can be stacked above the 5th to create intervals of 7ths, 9ths, 11ths, and 13ths. Again, these require more advanced study to understand thoroughly, but we will touch briefly on some terms you will hear

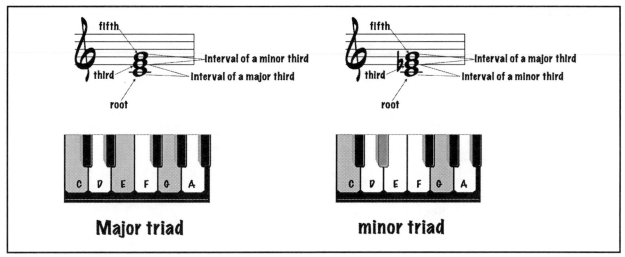

Figure 5.91 a and b: Triads are built of two intervals. Major triads have a major 3rd below and a minor 3rd on top. Minor triads have a minor 3rd below and a major triad on top.

regarding chords.

In sheet music or lead sheets, chords are notated using, unsurprisingly, *chord symbols*. Even if you do not fully understand what it means, you should know how to decipher parts of a chord symbol.

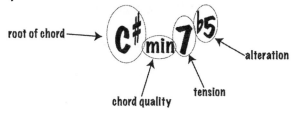

Figure 5.92: Parts of a chord symbol.

The parts of a chord symbol are:
Root – Bottom note (by letter name) of the chord.

Chord quality – Abbreviation to indicate the triad quality of the chord (major, minor, augmented, diminished, or sustained). If a chord symbol does not have one of these indicators, it is assumed to have major triad at the "base" of the chord.

Tensions or *extensions* above the triad – Arabic numbers indicate notes added to the triad: 6ths, 7ths, 9ths, 11ths, or 13ths, or alterations of these, such as ♭9, ♯9, ♯11, ♭13.

Alterations – Changes to the triad, especially the 5th. Usually indicated with a flat or sharp (see below for variations). There are many different abbreviations for chord quality. While some are clearer or more common than, others you should be able to recognize any of the written symbols in figure 5.93.

You cannot be expected to know the sound, the "spelling," or the emotional characteristic of all these chords, but if you read one out loud, you can pronounce it properly. See the Chord Translator at fig. 5.94.

One additional way that musicians refer to chords is by number. Generally, this refers to chords built on the scale degrees of the key being played (fig. 5.95). These chords have a particular harmonic function and are written with Roman numerals. They are pronounced by number: "the

Chord quality	Abbreviations	How you might see it written
Major	Maj, Ma, M or Δ	A Maj, B Ma, C#M, DΔ, Eb
Minor	min, mi, m, or -	E min, F#mi, Gm, Ab-
Sustained	sus 4, sus	Bb sus 4, C sus
Augmented	aug, +	D aug, E+
Diminished	dim, °	F dim, G°

Figure 5.93: Chord qualities of triads and the many ways they are written.

Symbol	Pronounced	Translation
Ab	A flat	A flat Major triad
B maj 7	B major seven	B major triad with a major 7th
C# min	C sharp minor	C sharp minor triad
D min 7	D minor seven	D minor triad with a minor 7th
Eb 7	E flat seven	E flat dominant 7 (Eb maj triad with a minor 7th)
F min 9	F minor nine	F minor triad with a minor 7th and a Major 9th
G# min 7 b5	G sharp minor seven, flat five	G sharp minor triad with a minor 7th and a diminished 5th

Figure 5.94: Chord symbol pronunciation and translation chart.

one chord," or "the flat-seven chord" or sometimes just "the five." If you are able to calculate the scale degree of a particular key, you can understand which chord is indicated.

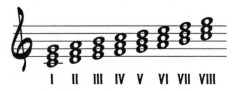

Figure 5.95: Chords built on each scale degree in a major scale, by number.

There are literally hundreds of possible chords, the study of which is a whole book in itself. As a start, ask a musician friend to play triads, 7th chords, and others while naming each as it is played, so you can begin to recognize their qualities. For a fuller understanding, take a music theory or ear training class, or search for free information on the Internet.

Lesson 9 Practical Exercise

A. Questions

1.   What is harmony?

2.   What is a triad?

3.   What are the five common triad qualities?

4.   How do we refer to the notes in most triads?

5.   From bottom to top, which intervals create a major triad? _____, _____

6.   From bottom to top, which intervals create a minor triad? _____, _____

7.   In the chord symbol below, what parts of the chord are F and Maj, respectively?

Fmaj7

Lesson 9 Practical Exercise

B. Visual Practice

Write out, in words, the pronunciation of the following chord symbols:

1. Bb7 _____B-flat seven_____

2. E min_____E minor_____

3. A# dim7_____

4. D _____

5. G maj7_____

6. C min7_____

7. F#+ _____

8. Bb° _____

9. E7#9 _____

10. A -7_____

11. DΔ7 _____

12. Gb _____

13. C -7b5 _____

14. F min _____

15. B dim _____

16. E aug _____

Chapter 6: Musical Instruments

What you should know:
How to identify, by sight and sound, the instruments most commonly used to make music

Why you should know it:
Musical instruments are the cornerstones of the recording process; they are, of course, what is being recorded. The various instruments' natural sonic characteristics and ranges provide a wide choice of timbres for writers and producers. Familiarity with instruments and their sounds is crucial to those who wish to use them for creative expression.

Lesson 10: Identifying Instruments

As we have seen in Chapter 1, use of some instruments rather than others is part of what defines genres. The creative decision of which instruments to use—both typical and atypical of a genre—is part of what helps writers, arrangers, and producers express themselves musically.

To deal in depth with all orchestral and band instruments is beyond the scope of this book. Our main focus will be identifying the instruments that are currently the most prevalent in a recording environment. It is suggested that the reader study a good orchestration book and listen to music from many genres and many eras to gain a better understanding of how various instruments are used.

To explore the many instruments involved in making music, we will look at them based on families of instruments: strings, woodwinds, saxophones, brass, percussion, and keyboards. We will also examine other groupings of instruments by type and by ensembles in which they are commonly played. The following pages give a brief introduction to several instruments in each family. Look at the pictures and listen to the CD tracks to gain basic familiarity with them.

The String Family

The Violin Family
There are four instruments in the violin family. All are made of wood, have four strings, and are commonly played by bowing, that is, drawing a bow—a long, slightly curved rod with horsehair stretched tightly between its ends—across a string. They can also be plucked with the fingers. Playing with the bow is called bowing or *arco;* plucking, which is less common, is called *pizzicato.*

Violin – the highest instrument in the family to which it gives a name. It is placed under the chin, somewhat to the side of the player while playing. When used in traditional, folk, or country music, the same instrument, played in stylistically different ways, is called a *fiddle*.

Track 32: Violin.

Track 33: Violin pizzicato.

Track 34: Violin played arco.

Viola – the second-highest instrument in the violin family. It looks like a violin but is slightly larger. It is held and played similarly to the violin, as described above.

Track 35: Viola.

Cello – the second-lowest instrument in the violin family. The player is seated while playing; the cello is placed between the knees and supported at its base by a peg that rests on the floor.

Track 36: Cello.

Bass or *Double Bass* – the lowest instrument in the violin family. Because of its size, the instrument stands on the floor and is rested against the player's shoulder while playing. The instrumentalist stands or sits on a stool to play the bass.
With all strings of the violin family playing long, *legato* (connected) notes, they can create a uniquely smooth, mellow sound, which is desirable in many genres.

Track 37: Orchestra Strings playing legato.

Track 38: Orchestral Strings playing staccato.

violin

viola

cello

bass

Figure 6.96: The violin family.

Guitars
Found in every type of modern popular music, the guitar is quite versatile. It is played as a lead instrument and in the background. Many bands have two guitar players, with one playing *lead guitar*—solo and "out front" parts—and the other playing *rhythm guitar*—strumming or playing patterns to help create the groove.

Acoustic Guitar – a hollow, wooden instrument, usually with a *sound hole* in the middle where the strings are played. There are two main types of acoustics: *nylon string* guitars and *steel string* guitars. Nylon string guitars (also called *classical* or *Spanish* guitars) are primarily used in classical or folk music. They are quiet and possess a mellow, intimate sound. Steel string guitars are louder and more piercing than nylon string guitars, but more intimate sounding than electrics. Some steel string guitars are fitted with electronics so that they can be plugged into amplifiers (see below). There is a wide variety of playing styles for guitars. The player can strum all of the strings at once, pluck 2 or more strings at a time, or pick one note at a time in a melody (lead), or in one of hundreds of patterns (rhythm part). Strings may be played with a flat pick, fingers, fingernails, or finger picks.

Track 39: Nylon string acoustic guitar, strummed, then picked.

Track 40: Steel string acoustic guitar, strummed, then picked.

Electric Guitar – a solid-bodied instrument with electronics built into the body to pick up the sound from the strings and play it through an *amplifier* or *amp* (device to boost the sound level). Without amplification, electric guitars would be very quiet, but with it, they can be among the loudest instruments.

Track 41: Electric Guitar, strummed, then picked.

The electric guitar can produce many different sounds, particularly when used with *effects*—electric or electronic devices that alter, increase, or cut components of the original sound wave. Digital processors can often perform the function of several effects units.

Track 42: Guitar with *chorus* effect.

Track 43: Guitar with *distortion*.

Track 44: Guitar with *wah wah* effect.

Track 45: Guitar with *echo* or *delay*.

Bass Guitar – is more commonly called *electric bass*, *E-bass*, or simply "bass." It is held like a guitar. It can be plucked with the fingers or a pick, or hit with the fingers. *Slapping* a bass can mean pulling a string so hard it bounces off the fingerboard or smacking all the strings with the fingers. *Popping* is hitting a string with the finger or a thumb. Slapping and popping, sometimes alternating between the two, produce distinctive percussive sounds.

Track 46: Electric Bass. Track 47: Upright Bass.

Acoustic or *Upright Bass* – This is the double bass (see violin family, above), but played in a different style. Prior to electric bass, it was a common rhythm section instrument. It has become much less common than electric bass, but is sometimes still played in jazz, swing, rock, and folk music. It is typically plucked or slapped, as a bass guitar is played.

acoustic (nylon stringed)

electric guitar

bass guitar

acoustic (steel stringed)

Figure 6.97: The guitar family.

Harp

There are various types of harps; the one typically used in orchestral and other settings is the *concert grand harp*. It has 47 strings stretched vertically across a large frame. The harpist sits with the instrument between the arms and legs, with the slanted side against one shoulder. A harp is plucked or strummed with the fingers of both hands. Seven pedals on the instrument are used to change the length of the strings, raising or lowering notes by a half step.

Track 48: Harp.

Figure 6.98: Concert Grand Harp.

Piano

While it fits into several categories, the piano *is* a stringed instrument. See Keyboard Instruments, below, for details.

Reed Instruments

Reed instruments are blown to make sound. Most of these instruments have a piece of thin cane—a reed—which vibrates in the current of air to produce the instruments' sounds.

The Woodwind Family

As one might guess from the name, woodwinds are instruments that are (traditionally) made of wood and are blown to make sound.

Piccolo and *Flute* – the highest and second-highest instruments, respectively, in the woodwind family. Originally made of wood, they are currently made of metal (and thus are non-wood woodwinds). Flutes and piccolos are the only woodwinds that do not have a reed to produce a sound. They are held to the side of the flutist, who blows air horizontally across a hole against an edge.

Track 49: Piccolo.

Track 50: Flute.

Oboe and *English horn* – with the clarinet, oboe and English horn are the middle-to-high range instruments in the woodwind family. Like the clarinet, they're made of wood and are played by blowing air into them. Unlike the clarinet, they are *double reed* instruments, that is, they have two reeds that vibrate to produce their characteristic sound. They are tuned in C.

Track 51: Oboe.

Track 52: English horn.

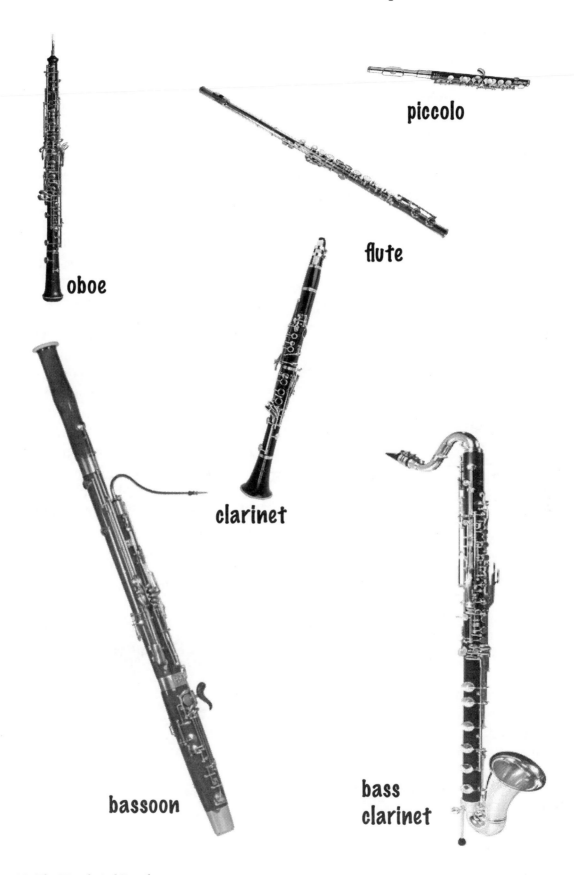

piccolo

flute

oboe

clarinet

bassoon

bass
clarinet

Figure 6.99: The Woodwind Family.

Clarinet and *bass clarinet* – middle-to-high and low-to-middle range woodwinds, respectively. They have the widest overall ranges in the woodwind family. Both are wooden, *single reed* instruments, that is, they have a thin piece of bamboo in the mouthpiece, which vibrates when air is blown into them. They are normally tuned in B flat, though some clarinets are tuned in A or E flat.

Track 53: (a) Clarinet and (b) Bass clarinet.

Bassoon and *contra bassoon* – the second-lowest and lowest instruments, respectively, in the woodwind family. The bassoon has approximately the same lowest notes as a bass clarinet, but lacks the higher range of a bass clarinet. The contra bassoon plays one octave lower than the bassoon. They are double reed instruments and are tuned in C.

Track 54: Bassoon.

The Saxophone Family

The saxophone, often called a sax, is a single-reed instrument made of metal. It is used in many types of music, especially jazz. Alto and tenor saxes are particularly versatile and used in concert and marching bands, theater orchestras, as well as the horn sections in rock and R&B bands.

Soprano Sax – the highest instrument in the saxophone family. Associated mainly with jazz or "smooth jazz" music, it uses a single reed to produce sound. It is tuned in B flat.

Track 55: Soprano sax.

Alto Sax – the second highest in the saxophone family. It is tuned in E flat.

Track 56: Alto saxophone.

Tenor Sax – the second lowest instrument in the family. It is tuned in B flat.

Track 57: Tenor saxophone.

Baritone Sax – nicknamed *bari sax*, this instrument is the lowest of the saxophones. It is tuned in E flat.

Track 58: Baritone saxophone.

Other Reed Instruments

Harmonica – a reed instrument very different from woodwinds or saxes, the harmonica is a small, hand-held metal instrument with a row of reeds inside it. The player moves the harmonica from side to side to play different notes by blowing or sucking air. Each harmonica has only the notes in a single major scale, so a player needs a different harmonica for every key. It is also called *mouth organ*, *blues harp*, or *French harp*.

Track 59: Harmonica.

Figure 6.101: Harmonica.

alto sax

soprano sax

baritone sax

tenor sax

Figure 6.100: The Saxophone Family.

The Brass Family

All modern brass instruments are played by blowing into a mouthpiece with closed lips, which vibrate, creating a buzz, which produces sound that is amplified by traveling through metal tubing. Pitch is always partially controlled by the pressure of air between the lips and the shape of the mouth.

Trumpet – the highest instrument in the brass family. This instrument is used in many styles and ensembles. In addition to air and lip pressure, pitch is controlled by closing and opening valves. The most common type of trumpet is tuned in B flat, though there are trumpets tuned to other keys. Orchestras often use C trumpets.

Track 60: Trumpet.

French Horn – the medium-low sound of the orchestral brass family. In addition to air and lip pressure, pitch is controlled by closing and opening valves. French Horns are tuned in F.

Track 61: French Horn.

Trombone – also a medium-to-low instrument in the brass family. In addition to using air and lip pressure, a trombone uses a slide to change pitch. The slide gives the trombone a unique ability to bend pitch.

Track 62: Trombone.

Tuba – the lowest instrument in the brass family. Like the trumpet and French horn, pitch is changed both with air and lip pressure and closing and opening valves.

Track 63: Tuba.

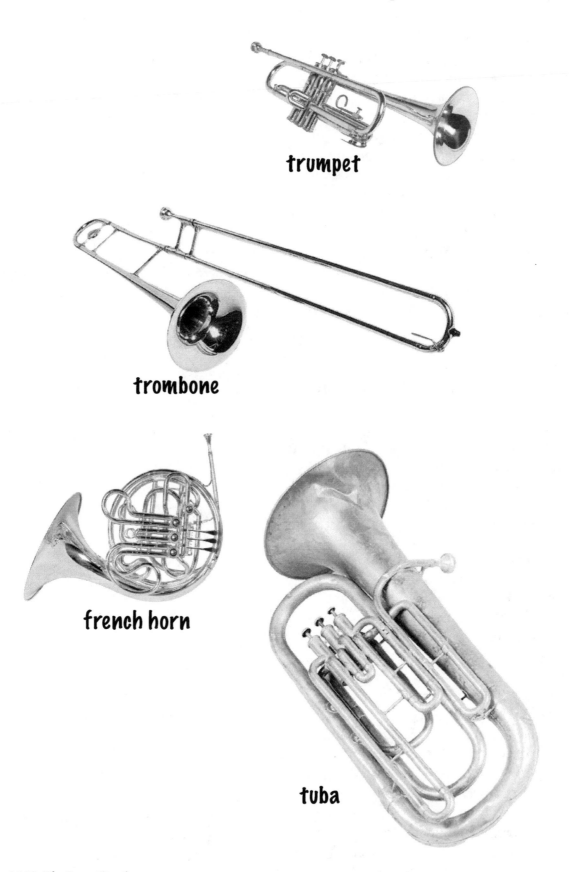

trumpet

trombone

french horn

tuba

Figure 6.102: The Brass Family.

The Percussion Family

Percussion instruments are those that make sound by hitting them with a hand, stick, mallet, or brush, or by shaking them. They are made out of a variety of materials. Percussion instruments are divided into two subcategories: those of *definite pitch*, also called simply *pitched* percussion, where particular notes can be heard when striking the instrument; or those of *indefinite pitch*. The drum set is of indefinite pitch, but as it consists of many parts and is frequently used in popular styles, it is presented as a separate category.

Definite Pitch Percussion

Timpani – also called *kettledrums* – are made of a skin stretched across a large bowl, often made of copper. They are struck with a mallet or beater. A timpanist plays at least two and up to four drums, which are commonly tuned in fourths.

Track 64: Timpani.

Xylophone, *Marimba,* and *Vibraphone* – each consists of a set of bars of varying lengths, tuned to different pitches and arranged in the same pattern as piano keys. Each is played with two to four mallets.

Xylophones and marimbas have bars made of wood, and are used in a variety of music, including classical, band music, folk, and contemporary Latin. The vibraphone, commonly called "vibes," is similar in construction to xylophones and marimbas, but has bars made of metal and a sustain pedal, which allows notes to be held longer or dampened. It also has a motor that rotates disks at the ends of resonating tubes. This mechanism creates its unique tremolo sound. Vibes are used occasionally in popular genres, but as a lead instrument are most common in jazz.

Track 65: Xylophone.

Track 66: Marimba.

Track 67: Vibraphone.

Tubular Bells or *Chimes* – thin, hollow metal cylinders hung vertically from a rack, arranged and tuned like the keys of a piano. They create a sound similar to distant church bells.

Track 68: Tubular Bells.

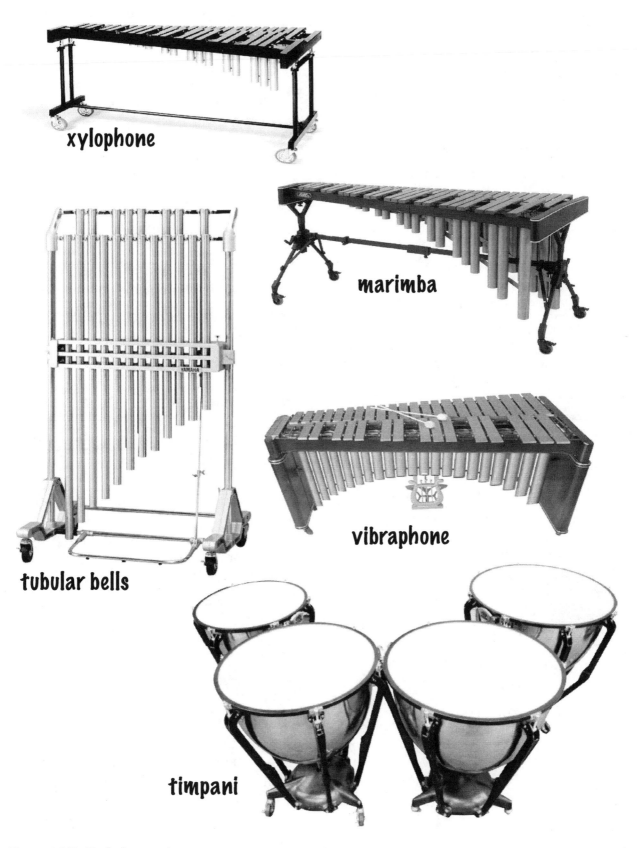

xylophone

marimba

tubular bells

vibraphone

timpani

Figure 6.103: Pitched percussion.

Percussion of Indefinite Pitch

This is a broad category. Anything that can make a sound by shaking or hitting it can be considered a percussion instrument. All genres of music, from classical to pop, have used non-traditional percussion. Chains, doorbells, wooden spoons, cardboard boxes, whips, and garbage cans have all been used creatively and successfully.

Snare Drum – two skins stretched across the top and the bottom of a low cylinder. The bottom skin has wire coils called *snares* stretched across it and attached to the edges of the drum to create a rattling sound that makes this drum distinctive. The snare can be turned off or on through the use of a lever which tightens or loosens the wires (see fig. 6.106, drum set).

Track 69: Snare Drum.

Bass drum – the largest percussion instrument. It is most common in orchestras and concert or marching bands. It can produce a sound like loud thunder, or like a heartbeat. It is made of two skins stretched on opposite sides of a wide cylinder. Unlike the kettledrum and snare, it is placed vertically, on its side, so that the player can strike either or both sides of the drum (see fig. 6.104: Orchestral percussion).

Track 70: Bass Drum.

Cymbals – round, thin plates of brass that can produce a sound similar to a crack of lightning, a splash in a pool of water, or the sound of wind. In an orchestra, concert band or marching band, two cymbals can be held, one in each hand, to be struck against one another (crash cymbals).

Cymbals can also be suspended and struck with mallets, sticks, or brushes (suspended cymbal). For set-specific cymbals see Drum Set, below (fig.6.106).

Track 71: (a) Crash Cymbal (b) Suspended cymbals.

Triangle – a metal rod that is bent to form a triangle. It is hit with another metal rod.

Track 72: Triangle.

Tambourine – a small hand drum with one head, or sometimes just a frame with no head. Metal discs are attached loosely around its circumference. The tambourine can be shaken, hit with the hand, or hit with a beater.

Track 73: Tambourine.   Track 74: Congas.

Congas – tall, narrow wooden drums with skin heads. They can be played sitting or standing, attached to a stand or held between the knees. Normally, two or three congas of slightly different sizes are played together. They are struck and slapped with the hands and fingers. Though common in Latin styles, congas are used in many other contemporary music genres.

Bongos – two small, connected drums of slightly different sizes. They are held between the knees and played with the hands and fingers.

Track 75: Bongos.   Track 76: Shaker.

Shaker – hand percussion instrument made of small beads in a closed container, often a metal tube. Can be rocked back and forth with the hand to create a soft, natural percussive sound, or can be shaken hard and rhythmically to create a crisp sound.

bass drum

suspended cymbal

crash cymbals

snare drum

Figure 6.104: Orchestral percussion.

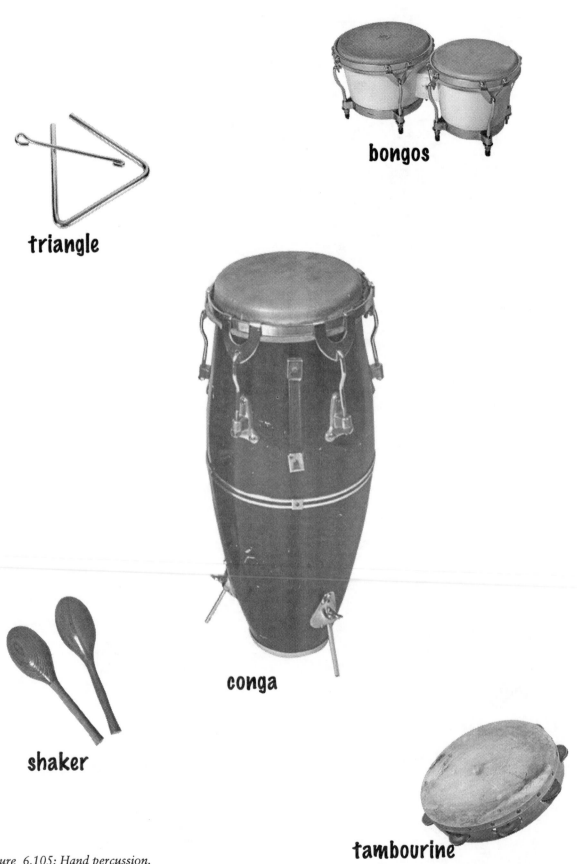

triangle

bongos

conga

shaker

tambourine

Figure 6.105: Hand percussion.

Drum Set

Sometimes called *drum set*, *drum kit*, *trap set*, or simply "the drums," virtually all recorded jazz and popular music has a drum set, its synthesized equivalent, or both. Along with the bass, it provides the foundation for most grooves. The drum set is a combination of various drums and cymbals. The drummer plays all of them simultaneously, typically with sticks or brushes. The specific instruments in a set will vary with genre and the player's preferences, but often include:

Snare Drum – fully described under "Percussion of Indefinite Pitch." This drum is a staple in popular music.

Track 77: Snare Drum.

Kick drum – The "real" name of this drum is bass drum, but it is frequently referred to as kick drum, or simply *kick*, which is convenient to distinguish it from the very different bass drum described above. The kick drum sits on the floor in front of the drummer and is struck with a mallet operated by a foot pedal with the drummer's right foot.

Track 78: Kick Drum.

High-hat – two small-to-medium-sized cymbals threaded on a pole and facing each other, one above and one below, that come together via a foot pedal mechanism operated by the drummer's left foot. The high hat is played with a drumstick or brushes while simultaneously being opened and closed. Along with the kick drum and snare, it provides the basis of the drum groove for most popular music. It is often the easiest sound to focus on to determine the smallest subdivision of the beat.

Track 79: High Hat.

Tom toms – sometimes called simply *toms*, these drums come in different sizes, from small to large. If a drum set has two or more (they often do), the toms are tuned from high to low. They have a slightly boomy sound and are often used for drum fills, to add emphasis, or for contrast to the snare.

Track 80: Tom toms.

Ride Cymbal: this large cymbal often maintains the subdivisions of the beat and is a foundation for the groove in swing or jazz. It is sometimes used instead of the high hat in popular styles as well.

Track 81: Ride cymbal and jazz groove played with brushes.

Crash Cymbal – as the name implies, this large, loud cymbal is used to provide crashing accents, often on the downbeat of a new song section, or for emphasis and excitement.

Track 82: (a) Crash and (b) splash cymbals.

Other pieces: a few of the many possible additions to the above might be splash cymbal, wind chimes, or hand percussion.

Track 83 Various drum set grooves: (a) Rock, (b) Blues, (c) Shuffle, (d) Jazz, (e) Funk, (f) Latin.

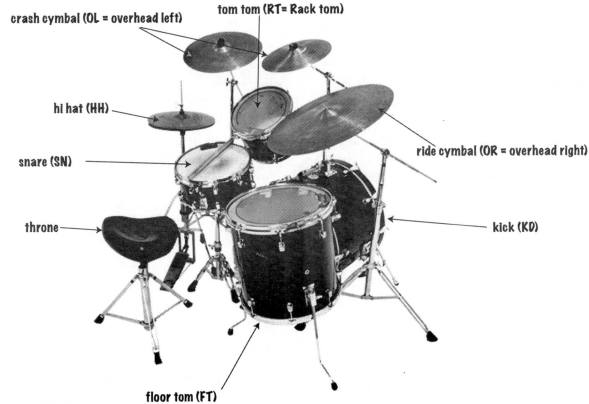

Figure 6.106: Drum Set.

Keyboard Instruments

Pianos, organs, and synthesizers as a group are often called *keyboards*, or simply *keys*. They produce sound in very different ways, but look similar: all have keys in the familiar black and white pattern and are played with all ten fingers of both hands.

Piano – considered both a string instrument and a percussion instrument because sound is created when the pianist plays a key, which operates a hammer, which strikes the strings of a given note. It has a very wide range and can create many different moods and stylistic grooves depending on how it is played. Due to this versatility, it is used in almost all genres of music. Since a piano has all the notes laid out in order, with one piano key per note, it is an excellent reference for those studying music and music theory (notice that it is used in this text). Advanced music students majoring in education or composition are generally required to have a certain level of competence in playing the piano.

▣ Track 84: Piano.

Electric Piano – also called *e-piano*. The sound of true electric pianos varies greatly due to various methods of tone production in different models. Some sound like tuned tines or forks; others sound more like traditional pianos or harpsichords. The most famous "classic" e-piano sound is a Rhodes piano. A synthesizer is often used to recreate the sound of true electric pianos.

▣ Track 85: Electric Piano.

Organ – a wind instrument which produces sound by forcing air through a set of tuned pipes. Organs have multiple tiers of keys, foot pedals (for very low notes), and levers or drawbars called *stops* to allow (or stop) different sets of pipes to sound. Pulling out stops alters both the volume and the tone of the overall sound. Modern organs may be pipe organs, electronic organs created to imitate pipe organs, or electronic organs with their own unique sounds. The latter is more common in the recording industry. The Hammond organ is one such organ. Its sound is considered "classic" and comes in and out of style for various popular genres.

Track 86: (a) Church Organ and (b) Jazz Organ.

Synthesizer – sometimes called simply a *keyboard*, or *synth,* a synthesizer has the capacity to produce imitated (electronically created) or sampled sounds. In can sound like a "real world" instrument, or like something out of this world. Further, a synth can play several different sounds at once; this is possible by the use of MIDI (Musical Instrument Digital Interface). MIDI is a protocol, or code, that allows electronic instruments to communicate with each other.

In addition to hardware synthesizers of the traditional type (i.e., with keyboards attached), there are also *sound modules* and *software synths*. These have the functionality of a "traditional" synth, but no keyboard. *Sound modules* are rack-unit synthesizers with all the functionality of a synth, but no keyboard. *Software synths*, also called *virtual instruments,* are computer programs with all the functionality of synthesizers.

Track 87: Synthesizers.

Sound modules and *software synthesizers* are synthesizers, but they may or may not have a keyboard of their own. If they do not, they must be connected to and triggered by either another synthesizer as a *MIDI controller* (keyboard that sends MIDI signals but has no sounds of its own), or a *sequencer* (device or computer program with multi-Track midi recording capability). A particular sound on a synthesizer, either pre-programmed by the manufacturer or created by a user, is commonly called a *patch*.

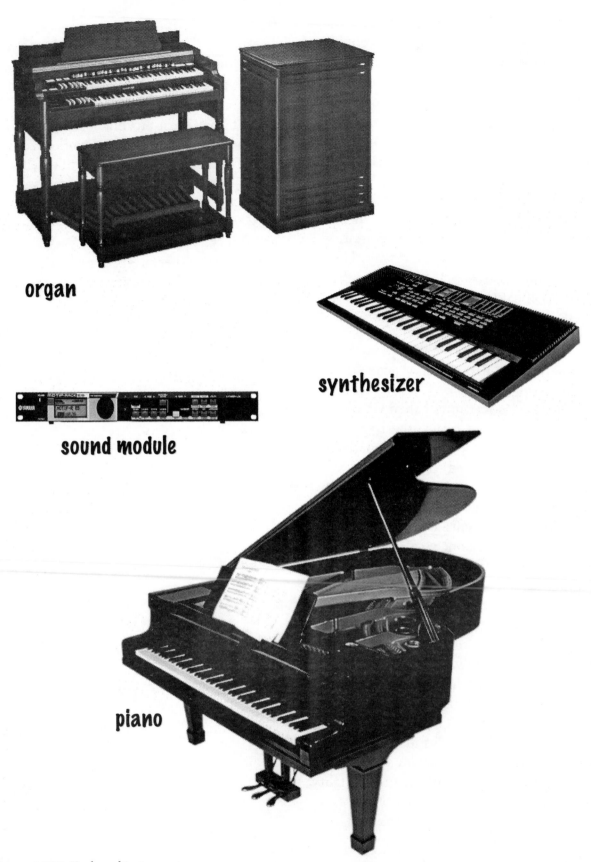

organ

synthesizer

sound module

piano

Figure 6.107: Keyboard instruments.

Human Voice

Singers are prevalent in all categories of music throughout the world. Though there are vastly different styles of singing and singers, voices are generally known by their ranges (from high to low): *Soprano, Alto, Tenor, Baritone,* and *Bass.* Soprano and Alto are parts generally sung by female singers; Tenors Baritone and Bass parts are sung by men.

Using the first letter of each vocal part, an acronym is created to describe music arranged for four-part vocals using all of these ranges: SATB. Musicians also use these terms for the different parts in any four-part writing, even if it's not for human voices. For example, they will refer to the 2nd highest part as the "alto voice."

Variant Instrumental Groupings

Sometimes you will hear terms that group instruments differently than by families. Some terms you should know include:

The Rhythm Section – Bass, drums, guitar, and piano or keyboard. May also include hand percussion or other rhythm instruments. This group of players establishes the style and groove of a song. Most ensembles will have bass and drums plus one or more of the other instruments mentioned (or, of course, the synthesized equivalent of any of them). The rhythm section is vital to all contemporary popular genres. Their playing is the nucleus of any band or arrangement.

Horns – in an orchestra, French horns. In popular bands, any saxophones, trumpets and trombones as a group are often called horns.

C Instruments – any instruments tuned in C.

Reeds – instruments with reeds, such as clarinets, saxophones, etc.

Ensembles – any group of musicians playing together can be called an ensemble. Large Ensembles include *orchestra, big band* (sometimes called *swing orchestra*), *choir,* and *concert band* or *marching band.* Large ensembles require a director or conductor to lead. Small and medium-sized ensembles in popular music are usually based on rhythm sections (see above), plus any combination of other instruments. Small ensembles might include four to six players, while medium-sized ensembles may have seven to fifteen players.

Duets – any two musicians playing or singing together.

Trios – any group of three musicians playing or singing together.

Quartet – any group of four musicians playing or singing together. String quartets and vocal quartets are fairly common.

Other musicians

In addition to those who play instruments, most projects require musicians with other musical skills and talents. These specialized abilities can be invaluable to producers, managers, and engineers.

Conductor, Director, or *Band Leader*
Though the term and specific duties vary for different genres and purposes, any large group of musicians needs an individual who oversees them and

insures a cohesive representation of a composition.

In classical music, this person is always the *conductor*. The conductor stands in front of the ensemble and directs with a *baton* (a long, thin pointer) and hand gestures. He or she will guide the tempo, give entrance cues, and shape the dynamics of the music. The conductor interprets the expression of the composer through the musicians.

In other genres, this function may be called *director* or *bandleader*. It may be a formal leadership position. For example, a choir director chooses music and rehearses the singers or musicians, then leads performances, but usually does not perform him or herself. A member of a band may be the individual who always manages and leads rehearsals, or it may be less formal, with duties shared between different band members, perhaps on different songs.

In a recording environment, this function depends on the number and type of musicians playing. For example, for horn or string arrangements, which require the musicians to sight-read their parts, the composer or arranger (see below) will likely conduct, even for as few as two or three players. For recording rhythm section players, a writer, arranger, music director, or band member might give direction. This might involve full conducting, counting off a tempo and cuing the ending, or giving general encouragement and suggestions to the players. The producer may perform some of the general functions of director, but will not conduct in the traditional sense.

Composer or *Songwriter* – someone who writes music and takes the elements of sound and puts them together in an expressive way. The end result could be a symphony, jazz score, opera, or a popular song.

Arranger – takes a song that is already written and: (a) writes specific parts (such as string or horn parts) to add style and interest to a recording, with chords and specifications from the composer or producer; (b) writes the entire score for all musicians for a performance or recording, perhaps for a tour or movie; or (c) re-works a song to make it fresh--sounding different from any previous recording of the song yet, recognizable as the original song. The arranger accomplishes this by changing the style of the tune, using different instruments, or changing rhythms and chords. This can involve writing out music as in definition (b), or by adding and removing parts, loops, and song sections, or layering or stripping out parts during the recording or mixing process. Thus, a contemporary producer is often acting as an arranger too.

Accompanist
When a vocalist or a solo instrumentalist is performing a melody, they need harmonic support. The accompanist (usually a piano or guitar player) plays the chords associated with the melody. Even if a singer or group will ultimately be on a recording with a rhythm section and full band, sometimes just a piano accompanist will be hired for rehearsals.

Lesson 10 Practical Exercises

A. Questions

1. Name 3 high-range instruments. _____, _____, _____.

2. Name 3 mid-range instruments. _____, _____, _____.

3. Apart from a bass, name 2 low-range instruments. _____, _____.

4. If the recording of an R&B track calls for "horns," name three instruments that might be used. _____, _____, _____.

5. Which instruments are commonly the basis of a rhythm section?

6. What is the word instructing a musician to play a member of the violin family with the fingers? And the word for returning to playing with the bow? _____, _____.

7. What are the three pieces of a drum kit that are commonly used to establish the groove in popular music? _____, _____, _____.

8. What kind of cymbal is often used to establish the groove in jazz music (and sometimes in popular music)?

9. Which family of instruments gets its sound started by the player "buzzing" his or her lips?

10. Name 2 single-reed instruments. _____, _____.

11. What does SATB stand for?

12. What kind of musician can you call to write string or horn parts for live players?

Lesson 10 Practical Exercises

B. Visual Practice

Identify and name these instruments.

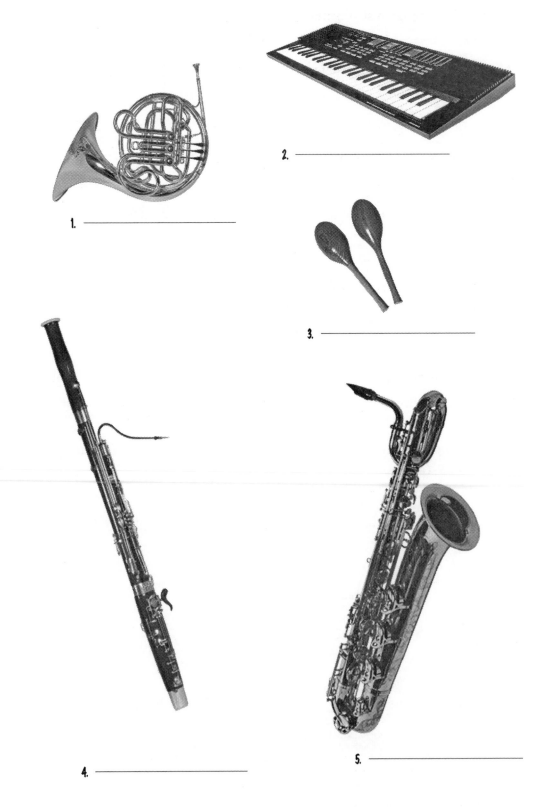

1. _____

2. _____

3. _____

4. _____

5. _____

Lesson 10 Practical Exercises

B. Visual Practice - 2

Identify and name these instruments.

6. _____

7. _____

8. _____

9. _____

10. _____

Lesson 10 Practical Exercises

C. Audio Practice

Listen to Track 88 and identify the instruments from their sounds.

Track 88: Instrument identification practice

1. _____

2. _____

3. _____

4. _____

5. _____

6. _____

7. _____

8. _____

9. _____

10. _____

Chapter 7: The Score

What you should know:
• The meaning of score markings
• How to follow along with written music while it is being played

Why you should know it:
A correct and clear lead sheet or score is critical to planning and organizing a performance by musicians or its use in recording sessions. It will enable all parties to know what is expected and help meet artistic objectives in an efficient manner, saving time and money. The ability to create and follow such a document is invaluable to give you more input into the performance and recording process.

Lesson 11: Score Expressions

Written expressions help the performer interpret the composer's intentions. They also show the "road map" of the music. The markings in the score also help musicians in rehearsal, when "let's make sure we're all on the same page" is not just a colorful expression.

In classical music, directions and expressions are of Italian origin, and are traditionally written in Italian. In popular music, it is acceptable to use English terms for some directions, as long as their meaning is clear. The main goal is that all players understand clearly what is meant. Apart from crucial information required of every piece of music (clef, key, and meter), the number of directions on music varies. There are benefits to both very detailed and very general notation. More direction means the writer can be more specific, especially if he or she has a very particular musical vision. But too many directions can be cluttered or confusing. The more specific the directions in the music, the less the writer is utilizing musicians' abilities to interpret the piece. Sometimes players can bring music to a higher level than the writer ever imagined.

In some situations, written music may not be needed—for example, if all players involved already know the music from memory. If a writer knows the musicians or if he or she is playing the piece, less direction may be needed. However, if players are reading or hearing the music for the first time, clear directions are crucial for successful execution of a performance.

Only a few score markings are written in their entirety. In order to facilitate the reading of music, and to save space and time—not to mention cost and inconvenience in copying and publishing—a system of abbreviations and symbols has been developed. Common abbreviations are given, along with their definitions.

Types of markings

Tempo

Tempo is the speed of the music, as discussed in Chapter 3. Tempo markings are given at the beginning of a song and any time there is a change in the speed. Tempo markings can be very specific, stating the number of beats per minute, and the value of a beat (see Chapter 3); this is also called the "Metronome marking."

Instructions on tempo can also be more general. Classical music has specific Italian words used to indicate the different *tempi* (plural of tempo) (fig. 7.108). These words are less specific than metronome markings and allow, within an accepted range, the conductor or musicians more freedom to move the music as it feels right to them.

Italian	Metronome	English Translation
largo, adagio	mm 40 to 50	very slow
andante	mm 60 to 90	moderately slow
moderato	mm 70 to 110	moderately
allegro	mm 120 to 160	fast, quick
presto	mm 150 to 190	very fast
accelerando, accel		get faster gradually
ritardando (ritard), rit		get slower gradually
rubato		irregular time (vary the tempo in an expressive way)
a tempo		back to original tempo (usually after a rit, or other tempo change)

Figure 7.108: Commonly used Italian tempo expressions.

The speed of music can change suddenly, at which time a new metronome marking or tempo expression would be written. However, it can also change gradually. *Ritardando*, abbreviated *ritard*, or simply *rit.*, is an order to slow down gradually. The order to speed up is *accelerando*, abbreviated *accel*. *Rubato* is irregular time. The soloist or conductor may play around with the tempo. The effect is usually emotional and dramatic (introductory verses, described in Chapter 2, are often *rubato*). After a *ritardando* or *accelerando* or *rubato* section, the score may tell the musicians to resume playing at the earlier tempo, indicated by "*a tempo*."

Feel or Timbre

After tempo markings, there may be instructions to play in a common stylistic way, e.g., "Swing 8ths" or "Swing 16ths." Sometimes these may be references to genre: *Bossa Nova*, *funk-rock*, etc., or a combination of style and genre: *loose funk*, or *jazz waltz*.

There are also instructions to indicate the character of a piece of music. They tell the musicians what "feel" or mood the music is to take. These are called *timbre directions*; some examples can be seen in figure 7.109. Sometimes timbre is a reference to emotions the writer wishes to inspire. Classical music is rich with these English words, like *joyously* or *lightly*, are also used effectively.

Feel, Style or Timbre	English Translation
♪♪ = ♪♪³	swing 8th
♫ = ♫³	swing 16th
con anima	with animation
con amore	lovingly
con brio	with brilliancy
con dolcezza	sweetly, with sweetness
con dolore	mournfully, with pathos
con forza	with force
con grandezza	in grand style
con gravita	with gravity
con legglerezza	lightly and delicately
con maesta	with majesty and grandeur
con molto espressione	very expressively
con molto passione	passionately
con moto	with motion
con precipitazione	in a hurried manner
con rabbia	furiously
con sentimento	with sentiment
	straight 8ths
	bossa or bossa nova
	swing
	rock
	funk
	joyously
	hip hopish

Figure 7.109: Timbre, feel, or style score expressions Dynamics.

Dynamics

Creative changes of volume are called *dynamics*. A common set of words and symbols to denote such changes is used by all musicians (fig. 7.110). Dynamic markings are labeled with the number 20 in the musical example fig.7.113.

Dynamic symbol	Italian expression	English translation
fff	fortississimo	very very loud
ff	fortissimo	very loud
f	forte	loud
mf	mezzo-forte	medium loud
mp	mezzo-piano	medium soft
p	piano	soft
pp	pianissimo	very soft
ppp	pianississimo	very very soft
sfz	sforzando	sudden, forceful accent
cresc.	crescendo	gradually louder
dim.	diminuendo	gradually softer
<	crescendo	gradually louder
>	decrescendo	gradually softer

Figure 7.110: Dynamics expressions.

Articulation and Expression These markings tell how to play a particular note or series of notes (fig. 7.111). The resulting difference in the sound of the music can be surprising.

So that you can see the expressions in context—as actually used in music—all symbols are numbered, with corresponding labels in figure 7.113 (see lesson 12).

Symbol, abbreviation	What it is	What it means	See fig. 7.113 numbers:
(phrase marking symbol)	phrase marking	play notes under the phrase with one breath or one stroke, or one bow direction etc... (much like a sentence with a comma)	35
—	legato	play note smoothly (long not short)	30
.	staccato	play note short (short not long)	15
>	accent	play note with force	38
v ʌ	vertical accent	also play note with force a little less than above	29
)	drop , dive or fall	drop both pitch and volume of note fading out	17
{ or gliss.	glissando	slide either into a note, away from a note or from one note to another	31
⌁ or tr..	trill	flutter between pitches a Maj.2 or Min.2 apart	34/41
♪	grace note	(note is smaller than other notes on the page) short note quickly, usually slurring into the next note	36
div.	divisi	divide (one person plays/sings the top note, the other takes the bottom)	22
non-div.	non-divisi	do not divide - the opposite of divisi (for string players both players play both notes at the same time)	25
Uni.	unison	unison (2 or more musicians play a single line together)	26
a2	A due, (in two parts)	play together (2 musicians play the same notes) often after a solo or divisi passage	50
𝄞 or 8va⌐	octave up	play one octave higher than written	47
𝄢 or 8vb⌐	octave down	play one octave lower than written	37
⌢ ⌣	fermata	hold note longer than its normal beat count	45
	tutti	all play or sing (often after a solo or duet)	
	tacet, (instrument(s))	silent, do not play, (specific instrument(s))	
	tacet	not play	
	a cappella	without accompaniment (vocals only)	
	poco	little	
	poco a poco	little by little	
	molto	much, very	
	con	with	

Figure 7.111: Articulations and other expressions.

131

Instrument-specific Expressions

There are many instructions that can be followed by some or most instruments. Other instructions are particular to one instrument or group of instruments, as described at fig 7.112.

symbol, abbreviation	What it is	What it means
N.C.		no chord (mostly to piano or guitar players)
pizz	pizzicato	(to string players) pluck with fingers
arco	arco	(to string players) return to bowing (after a pizz section)
shake or ᗺᗺᗺ	shake	(to brass players, or singers imitating brass) alternate quickly between pitches similar to trill, but usually a wider interval, up to a 3rd
o (+)	open close	(to brass) open or close plunger, creating a "wah wah" sound (to drummers) play open/closed high hat
trem. or ⪪	tremolo or roll	rapidly repeated note, especially for strings also used to notate drum roll
⊓	down-bow	(to string players) play by drawing bow downward
V	up-bow	(to string players) play by drawing bow up

Figure 7.112: Instrument-specific expressions.

Lesson 11 Practical Exercise
A. Questions

1.   What does largo tell the performer to do?

2.   Write a tempo marking which means, "In 4/4 time, play at 120 beat per minute."
_____.

3.   Musically speaking, how are "increase speed" and "decrease speed" written?
_____, _____.

4.   What does *a tempo* (the Italian expression) tell the performer to do?

5.   What kind of markings are "forte" and "piano"? How are they abbreviated and what do they mean?

6.   What does ♩♩ = ♩♩♩ tell the performer to do?

7.   Staccato, legato, and accents are common examples of what type of score expression?

8.   What does "guitar tacet" mean?

9.   What type of instrument might get pizz. or arco as a score instruction? What is the player being asked to do?

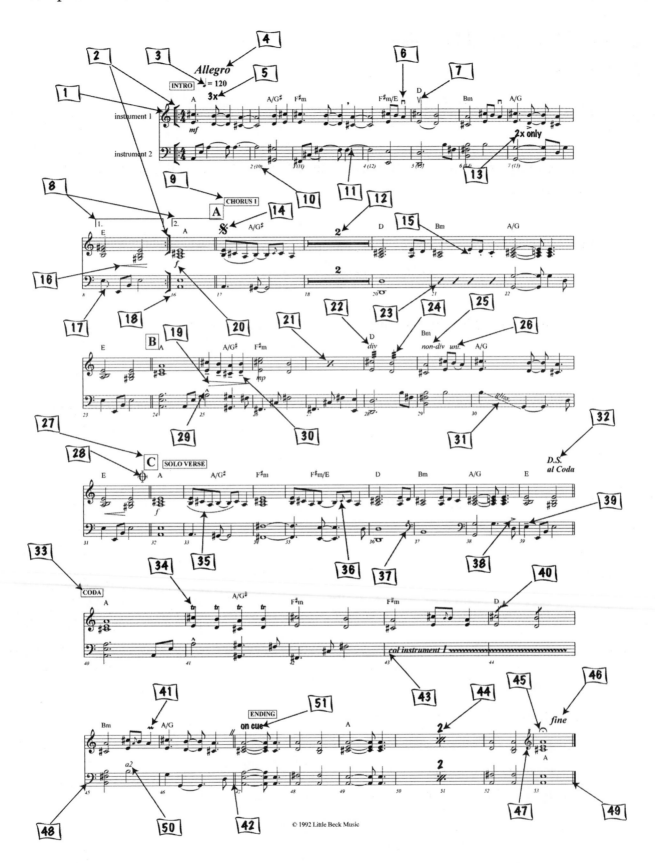

Figure 7.113: Score expressions in use. See the chart (fig. 7.111 and 7.114) for reference.

Lesson 12: Following the Music

Directions: the Road Map of the Music
An entire set of symbols and instructions direct the musician where to look and when.

Rehearsal letters are large capital letters, often in a box, used to identify sections of a song. When using written music, rehearsal letters become the signposts that everyone will look for (and quickly find) to ensure they are in the same place at the same time. They are crucial for efficient management of all involved in playing music together.

Measure numbers are placed at every measure (or in some cases, the first measure of every line). They're small numbers positioned at the beginning of the measure (either above or below it) in lead sheets, sheet music, or parts. On full scores, they're often large numbers, placed in the middle of the measure at the bottom of the page. Measure numbers should never be positioned at the end of measures, as it causes confusion.

Repeats If a section is played the same way twice, it generally won't be written out twice; instead a *repeat* symbol will be used to tell everyone "go back and play this part again." Repeat symbols are placed on both ends of a section to be repeated. They consist of two parts, one that says "go back" and the other, actually placed first in the music, that says "to here." After playing the section the 2nd time, where musicians play next depends on the repeat. If there is no additional instruction, it is understood musicians should go on to the next bar (fig. 7.114).

Some repeats may have text instructing the players to **Play 3x** (play three times). After the third time through, they then go on to the next bar or section. Sometimes a repeat may involve only one measure for one player. In this case, a measure repeat ℅ is written in the center of a measure to say "play the same thing as in the last measure." For two measures, the ℅℅ symbol is placed between two empty measures to say "play the same thing as in those last two measures."

Repeats may have different *endings* to a section. *First endings* have a bracket across the top of the measure(s) of the ending. The bracket is open on the left side. The number 1 is written at the "opening" of the box. The bracket "closes" at the end of the measure with the repeat sign. *Second endings* have a similar shape with the opening of the bracket to the right. There are special repeat instructions that involve skipping back to a measure or skipping ahead (past material already played the first time) to a new section. These are, respectively, the *Segno* 𝄋 and the *coda* ⊕ . A list of symbols, directions, and translations is at fig 7.114. However, musical directions only mean something in their proper context. Especially with symbols, it is best to see them on a piece of music. Go back to figure 7.113 to get an idea of how they might be used.

Types of written music
This is a more thorough discussion of different types of written music than the one in Chapter 1. You should be familiar with what is—and isn't—included in each of these:

Lyric sheet – just the lyrics to the song,

Symbol	What it is called	What it tells you	See fig. 7.113 number:
1, 2, 3, 4 etc.	measure numbers	(above or below measures) particular location in music	10
Ⓐ Ⓑ	rehearsal letters	(at beginning of sections of music) make it easier for all to find their places, for director to give instructions	27
⁒	1-bar repeat	play the last measure again	21
⁒⁒	2-bar repeat	play the last two measures again	44
⊢⊣	multi measure rest	(usually found in players' extracted parts) with a number over it, indicates the number of measures a player should not play. Saves ink and paper by representing silence for many measures in the space of one or two measures.	12
‖: :‖	repeat sign	when arriving at the right bracket, go back to the left bracket and play the whole section again	2
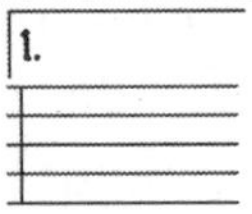 1.	1st ending	play the measure under the line "1." until arriving at a repeat sign (back repeat), then play section again (see 2nd ending)	8
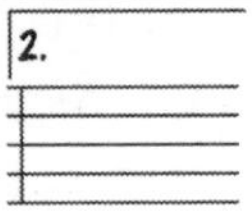 2.	2nd ending	the 2nd time through, skip measures(s) under 1st ending and jump to this measure and continue	8
D.C. or D.C. al	Da capo (al)	"to top", go back to the beginning of the piece (until....) Often followed by al Coda or al Fine	(see #32)
D.S. or D.S. al	Dal Segno (al)	jump (backward) to the sign (see below) until.... Often D.S. al 𝄋 or D.S al Coda (⊕) or D.S. al Fine	32
𝄋	Segno	"the sign" used to mark a specific location in music	14
⊕	Coda sign	jump (forward) to the coda sign (usually an ending section or movement	28
‖	double bar	usually used to separate sections	42
⫼	end bar	end of song or movement 9 often accompanied by Fine	49
2x (or 3x, 5x)	play 2 times (or 3,5 etc)	used to indicate the number of time to repeat a section between repeat signs	5
1x only (or 2x etc.)	play first time only	usually associated with a repeated section and indicates play this part the (x)th time through, but no other time	13
	vamp	play a section usually 1 to 4 measures, repeatedly, usually until a cue	
	on cue	play when signaled by director or soloist	51
Fine	Fine (FEE-nay)	end	46

Figure 7.114: Chart of score directions, i.e. "road map". symbols.

probably hand-written by the artist. For a rapper, this may be some ideas for the session, as a guideline for improvisation, or possibly the whole thing. Some players use these with lyrics written out in sections, chord symbols written over the words, and/or other notes about the piece.

Sheet Music – commercially-printed music with the melody on one staff, fully-written piano accompaniment on a grand staff, and chord symbols above (fig. 7.116). May have guitar chord notation. Sheet music is seldom shorter than two or three pages. Popular songs are often four or five pages long.

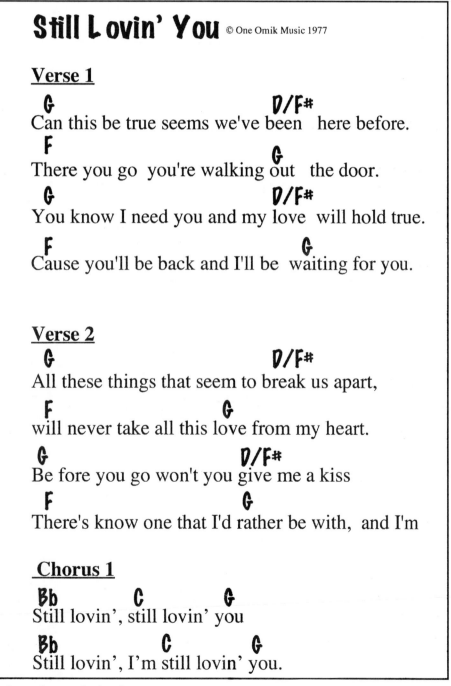

Figure 7.115: Lyric sheet with chords.

Figure 7.116: Sheet music, with vocal melody and words, plus fully written piano part.

Lead sheet – Melody, chords, and lyrics of a song all on one staff. Any rhythm section player has to comp (make up) his or her part when reading a lead sheet. Occasionally will have other directions or brief sketches of instrumental or background parts. Ideally, lead sheets are one or two pages long, but can be longer. For a typical set of lead sheets, used by many musicians, see *The New Real Book* series (fig.117 and 118).

Figure 7.117: Hand-written lead sheet.

Figure 7.118: Printed lead sheet.

Score – All the players' parts, as written by the arranger, used by the conductor, (see fig 7.119).

Parts – these are the individual players' parts copied (or extracted) from the score so that the players have only their own parts in front of them to read. This saves paper and eliminates extra information that the players don't need. Parts commonly come in two varieties:

1) *Parts* – actual music with all notes and score information written in (see fig. 7.120).

2) *Chord Chart* or *Zebra Chart* – the type of part that may be given to rhythm section players. A chord chart often has only the bare bones of the arrangement: repeats, rehearsal numbers, and codas, plus chords, slash marks, rests, and kicks over time, (see fig. 7.121) and explained below.

Slash marks ✓✓✓✓ are indicators that a player should comp. An arranger may write style instructions or a few bars of a sample of what he'd like, then slash marks, which in essence say, "You know what's best; play what grooves." The success of this type of part depends on the skill of the player(s).

Kicks over time are written rhythms (often written on the staff above slash marks) that tell an instrumentalist to play a certain rhythm on a specific beat. It usually does not tell a drummer which cymbal or a piano player which notes to play, just when to play an emphasized part.

Special concerns

If a score is written to be played with a MIDI sequence, time code, or SMPTE (a time code used in film scoring - SMPTE stands for Society of Motion Picture and Television Engineers), the score may need to have the code, or time, in minutes and seconds written in along with measure numbers. Repeats in such situations are considered new material and measures may have *two* measure numbers so that the engineer can follow (because recording is linear, of course). The same numbering system applies when using a segno or coda.

If SMPTE is used, the correct time should be added to the score at each rehearsal letter and at distinctive musical points in the score (fig. 7.122). See Appendix A for additional score preparation suggestions.

Following the score

To follow a score, you must first be able to find the beat at the correct tempo then visually keep pace with the music as it is being played. Conductors need to follow the overall sound of all players together, as well as all the intricacies of the performance of each player (no small task). Engineers, producers, and managers need only follow the pulse of the music so that they know where in the score the musicians are looking and playing.

The following process is recommended:

1. Choose one staff that you will follow throughout the score (on a lead sheet or chord chart there is no choice, as there is only one staff). Usually it's best to follow the top or bottom part.

2. Before a session or rehearsal, check the score for repeats. Put a tab of some type (paper clip, folded piece of tape) at the top

of the page at all repeat signs, including segnos and codas.

3. Number all the measures of the music. Treat repeats consistently. Either always count the measures that are to be repeated, or never count them.

4. Label song forms on the score (e.g., Verse 1, Verse 2, Chorus 1, Guitar solo, etc.). Engineers and producers can then indicate special recording directions (e.g., "add delay"). If needed, they might also indicate SMPTE time at specific sections.

5. When the music starts, tap your feet with the beat while you follow the score with your finger, pointing to the measures as they pass. As simple as this sounds, most people lose their places at some time or other, especially while learning. It is important to learn to listen to the music as it continues and find your place again. Wait for a specific section to come up and start counting from there.

Following the music takes lots of practice to be useful. During a recording session you must be able to focus on your main task of getting the music recorded correctly. You cannot be consciously thinking about tapping your foot or how the rhythm is subdivided; it must be second nature.

At the end of this chapter there are scores that correspond with CD tracks. Practice with the examples in this book, then practice with recordings and scores of other music. Mozart symphonies, Duke Ellington big band compositions, direct transcriptions, or sheet music for pop songs can be useful for learning to follow a recording.

Conclusion

I hope that through this book I have brought a sense of curiosity to those of you who may wish to study music in the future. Remember that we have only touched the surface of this discipline. My goal was to provide enough core information about music so that you can apply it to areas of music management, music recording, music production, and music performance. I will have achieved this goal if you are able to communicate more effectively and efficiently using the language of music.

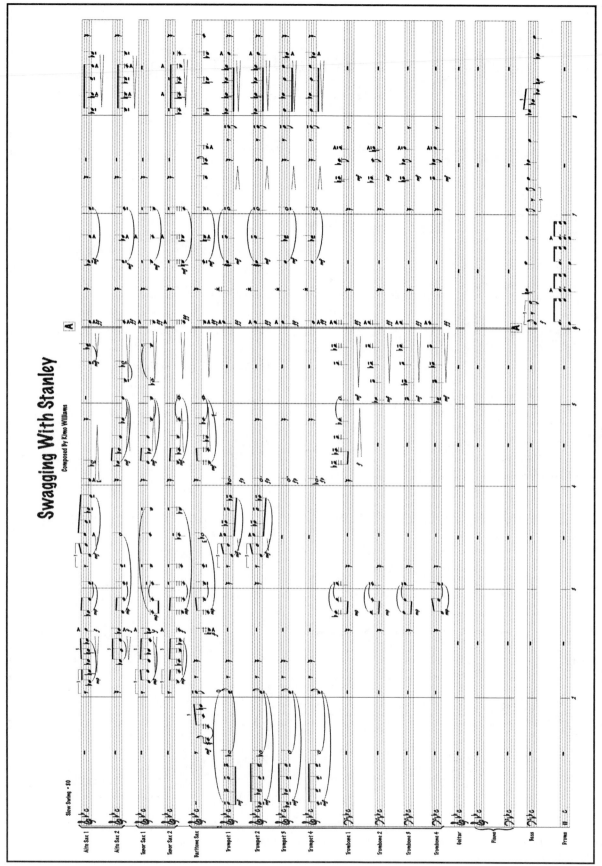

Figure 7.119: Full conductor's score (reduced). Scores are, obviously, much longer. To see multiple-page scores, see Appendix A.

Figure 7.120: Individual part. In this case, a horn part. These are extracted or copied from the larger score for just the players in question.

144

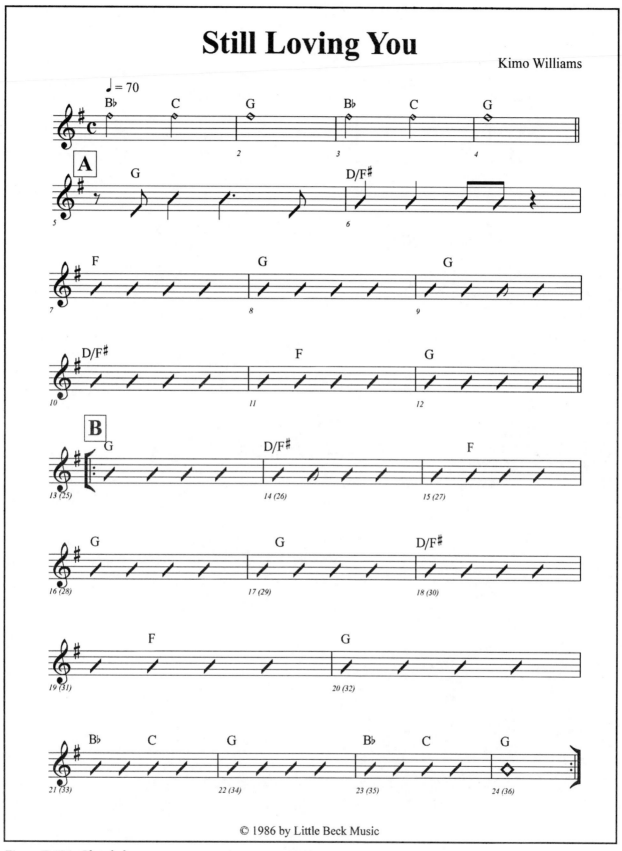

Figure 7.121: Chord chart.

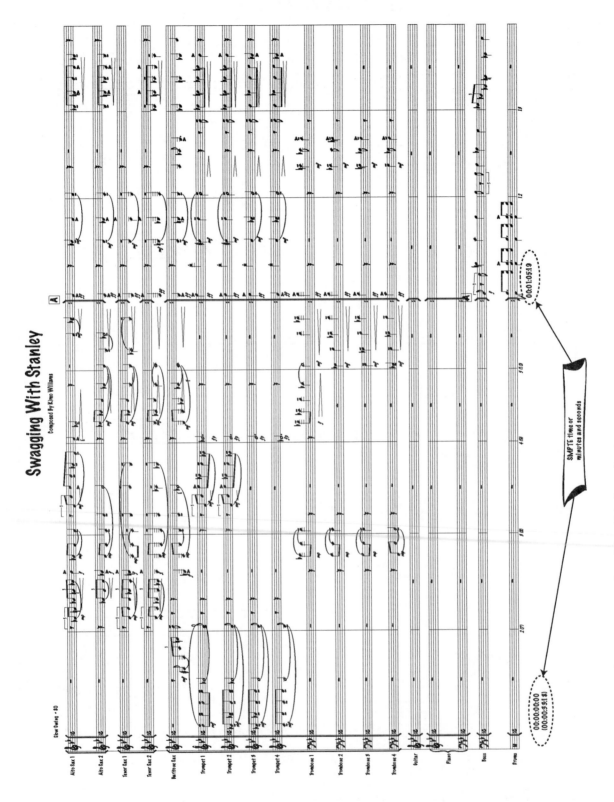

Figure 7.122: Score page with measures numbered for digital production.

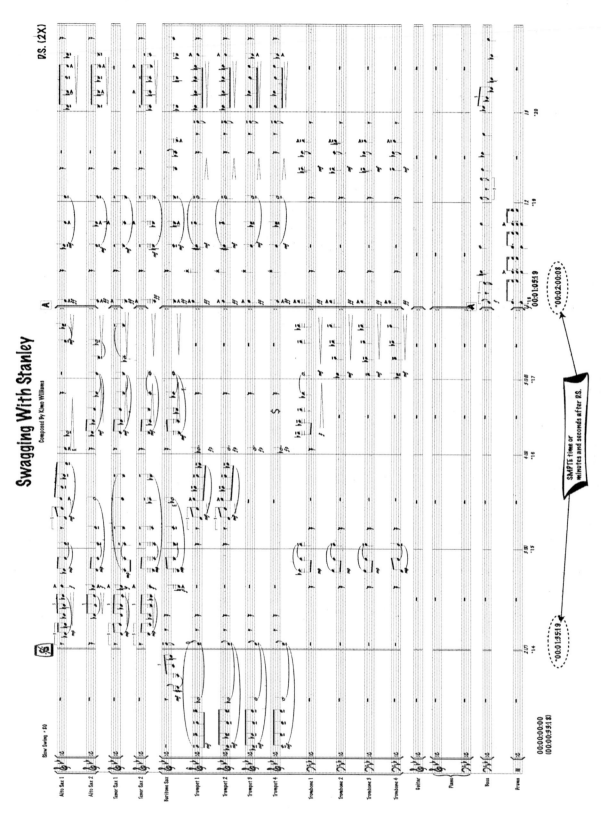

Figure 7.123: Score with time code and measure numbers for a D.S. or D.C. for digital production.

Lesson 12 Practical Exercise

A. Questions

1. What does D.S. tell the performer to do?

2. What does > (over a note) tell the performer to do?

3. What does D.C. al Coda tell the performer to do?

4. Describe typical rehearsal letters. Why are they important?

5. What are these: ✓✓✓✓? In what type of written music might you find them? And what do they tell the performer to do?

B. Visual Practice

Match the musical symbol with the score direction it represents:

1. %.   _____   a. multi measure rest

2. [1.] _____   b. 2nd ending

3. ‖:   _____   c. repeat sign ("go back")

4. :‖   _____   d. end barline

5.   _____   e. 1st ending

6. 𝄋   _____   f. forward repeat (start of repeated section)

7. D.C. or D.C. al _____   g. Coda sign

8. ⊢⊣   _____   h. repeat music from last measure

9. [2.] _____   i. the sign

10. ⊕   _____   j. go back to the beginning

148

C. Score following exercises

Figures 7.124 – 7.129 are scores for practice.

Play the CD that came with this book.

Select the tracks indicated at the top of each score and follow the written score while listening.

Each track has a count-off of "1 – 2 – 3 – 4 – " to give you a tempo and a place to start.

To help keep your place in the music, it may help to mark or highlight certain events:

• Places where instruments are entering for a particular section.

• Measure numbers.

• Locations of tempo change, as, of course, it will affect counting.

Count along and practice following in the music while listening. It may take several times through before you feel confident that you are in the right place in the music at the same time as the instruments. Next try following the line for only one instrument. Focus on listening to just that particular instrument's part while counting.

When the music ends, check to see where you are. Write the measure that the music stops in the blanks below. The answers are at the end of the book in Appendix B.

1. Symphonic practice score: Figure 7.124, Track 89. Ends in measure _____.

2. Jazz practice score: Figure 7.125, Track 90. Ends in measure _____.

3. Folk-pop practice score: Figure 7.126, Track 91. Ends in measure _____.

4. Chamber music practice score: Figure 7.127, Track 92. Ends in measure_____.

5. ¾ time practice score: Figure 7.128, Track 93. Ends in measure _____.

6. Symphonic full score: Figure 7.129, Track 94. Ends in measure_____.

Figure 7.124: Classical practice score. Follow along while listening to Track 89.

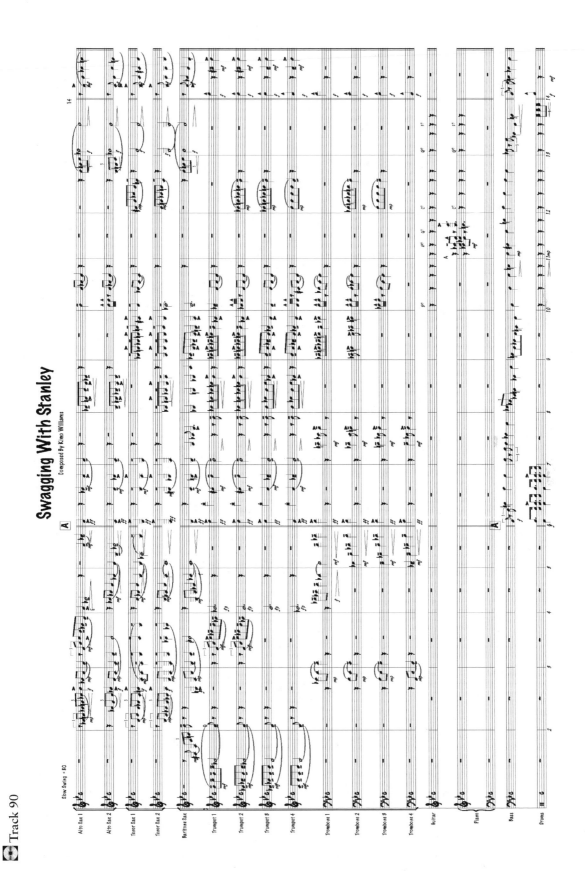

Figure 7.125: Jazz practice score. Follow along while listening to Track 90.

NEW YORK CITY LULLABYE

CAROL WILLIAMS

Figure 7.126: Folk-pop practice score. Follow along while listening to Track 91.

Two Gether

Duration 14:00

James Kimo Williams

Figure 7.127a: Chamber piece practice score (p. 1 of 2). Follow along with Track 92.

Figure 7.127b: Chamber piece practice score (p. 2 of 2).

Figure 7.128: Practice score in ¾ time. Follow along while listening to Track 93.

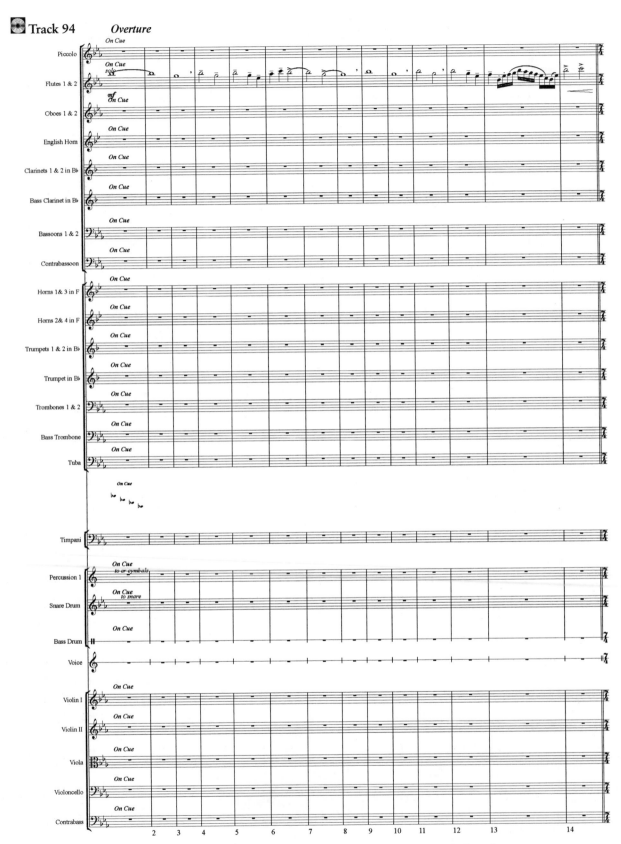

Figure 7.129: a-j (p 1 of 10): Symphonic practice score. Make sure the score is marked so that you can easily see new sections. Make sure the pages turn easily. Follow along while playing Track 94.

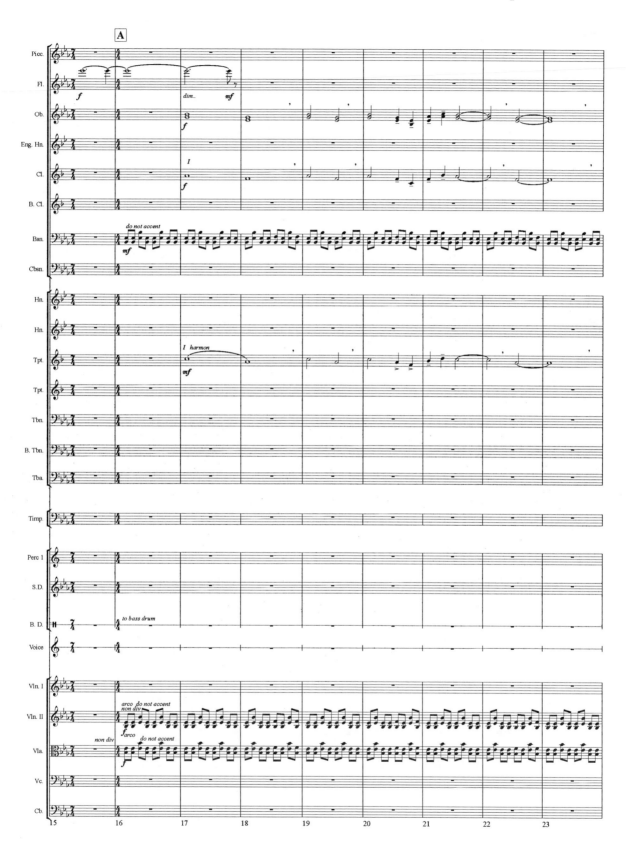

Figure 7.129: p 2 of 10.

Figure 7.129: p 3 of 10.

Figure 7.129: p 4 of 10.

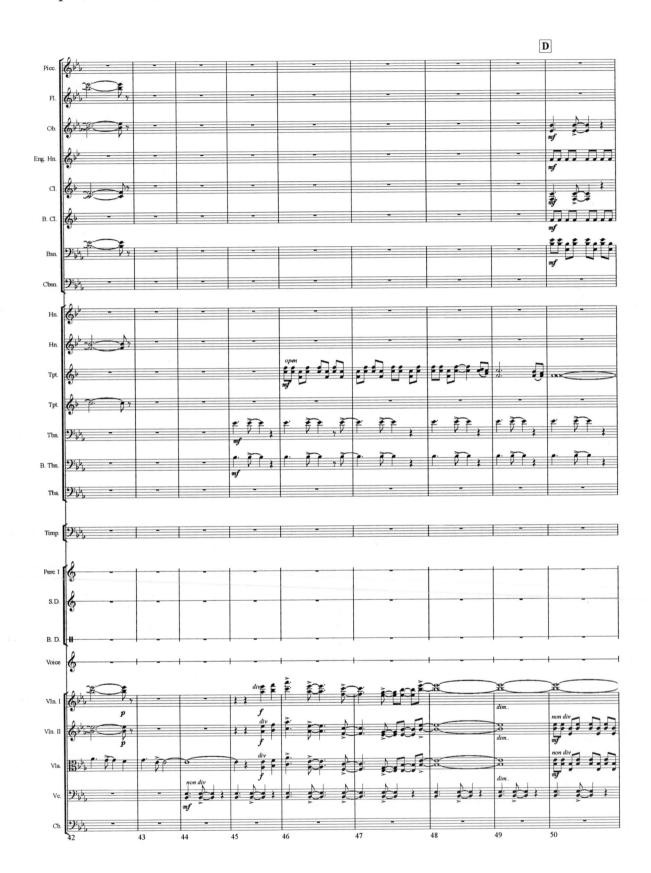

Figure 7.129: p 5 of 10.

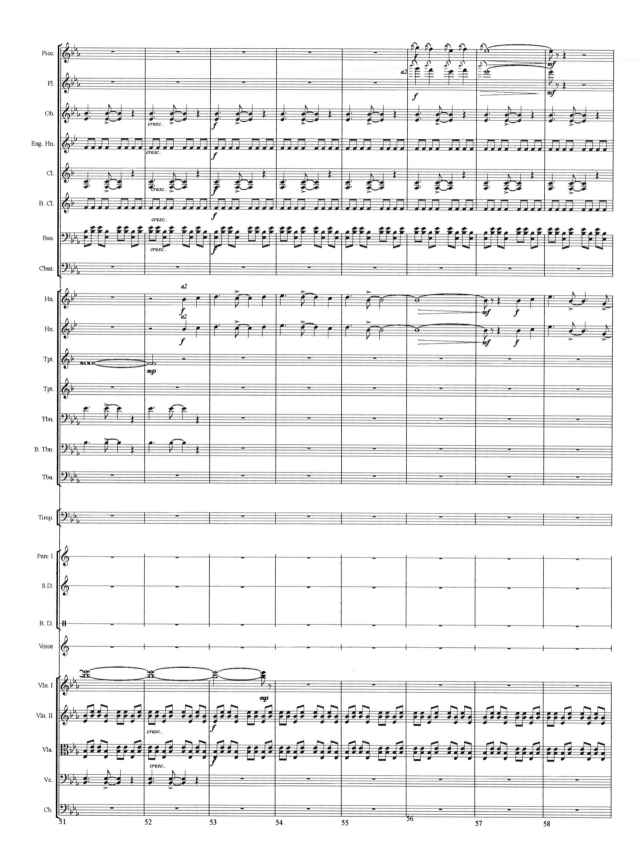

Figure 7.129: p 6 of 10.

Figure 7.129: p 7 of 10.

Figure 7.129: p 8 of 10.

Glossary

Terms a MEPA should know.

A

a cappella performed by voices only, without musical instruments.

a tempo back to the original tempo.

Absolute music the opposite of Program music. Music that is not connected to any predefined subject manner.

accelerando get faster.

accent an emphasis given to a note, usually with a volume increase and shorter duration.

accidental a sign or symbol indicating that a specific note is to be played as a flat, sharp, or natural.

accompaniment the harmonic support of a melody.

acoustics (1) the science of sound.(2) the description of how sound reacts within a space.

adagio a very slow tempo.

allegro a fast tempo.

alt-; alternative outside the current mainstream, but still within a genre, e.g. alt-country.

alto (1) the lowest female voice; (2) the second-highest voice in four-part chord writing; (3) the second highest instrument in the saxophone family.

ambience the aesthetic of a given space.

andante a moderately slow tempo.

aria a song piece in opera, usually for a solo performer.

arpeggio a chord whose notes are played successively rather than simultaneously.

arrangement (1) all the musical decisions made about the performance or recording of a piece of music; (2) an orchestration of a piece that gives it a different sonic character.

articulation how notes of a melody are connected or separated.

atonality; atonal music with no tonal center.

attack a part of the sound envelope that refers to the time it takes for a sound to achieve maximum amplitude.

avant garde new, experimental or outside the norm.

B

balance (1) the relative levels of the left and right channels of a stereo recording; (2) the relative levels of instruments or voices in a mix.

bar the meter of music divided on a staff (see measure).

baritone (1) a male voice of moderately low range; (2) the lowest instrument in the saxophone family.

bass (1) the lowest male voice; (2) the lowest instrument in the string family. Also called: stand-up bass; acoustic bass; string bass, upright bass and double bass; (3) the electric bass guitar.

bass clef the clef in the lower staff of the Grand Staff that shows pitches mainly for bass instruments and voices.

Big Band (1) a type of musical ensemble, originating in the 30's and 40's as a dance band. Consists of reeds, brass instruments and rhythm section. 12 – 24 players in all. Sometimes called a Swing Orchestra; (2) jazz music played by such a band. Sometimes called Big Band Swing.

blue note an alteration of certain pitches of a standard scale; especially a minor 3rd where a major third would be. Often this implies a note that is between standard half steps on a piano, but still used to musical effect.

bluegrass an early off-shoot of country and traditional music influenced by blues, jazz and gospel. Involves high vocal harmonies and extensive improvisation on guitars, banjos, mandolins, upright bass and fiddles.

blues a style of music that came out of the Black secular songs and field hollers, generally about longing or sad subjects. Influenced all popular music that came after it.

boogie-woogie a style of rhythmic jazz or blues piano, usually with repeating patterns in the bass and improvised patterns in the treble.

bop (short for bebop) a style of improvised jazz characterized by small group interactions and complex rhythm and harmony.

bow a rod with horse or fiber hairs tightly stretched from one end to the other. These hairs, when drawn over the strings of a violin, viola, cello or bass, produce sound.

BPM; bpm Beats Per Minute.

brass the family of wind instruments that uses a mouthpiece and is made of brass.

C

cadenza a virtuosic, often improvised section of a solo movement.

calypso a genre of syncopated music from the West Indies. Associated with fun in the sun.

call and response a performance style originating in Africa in which groups of performers, or a soloist and group of singers, alternate performing.

canon musical imitation, where one voice imitates another at staggered time intervals, such as "Row, Row, Row Your Boat."

CDR a Compact Disc on which one can record.

CDR Burner a device used to record data to CDR's.

celesta a keyboard instrument with hammers that strike resonating steel plates to produce a bell-like sound.

chamber music music played by small ensembles, such as a string quartet. During the 18th and 19th centuries, this music was played in the chambers of wealthy European patrons of the arts.

chorus (1) same as choir; (2) in standard AABA song form, the entire AABA pattern; (3) in popular song form, the repeated, often most memorable song section that follows the verse(s).

chord a group of notes played together

chord progression a series of chords played as the harmonic framework of a piece of music. Chords are to music what a plot is to a movie or book.

chromatics (1) pitches that are a semitone apart; (2) notes outside a given key or scale.

chromatic scale a succession of 12 pitches that are a semitone apart.

clef a symbol at the beginning of a staff that identifies the pitches located on the lines and spaces.

click track an audible metronome usually recorded on a separate track and provides the musician a way of keeping accurate time.

coda the ending section of a song or composition.

concerto a composition that features a solo instrument, or a small group of instruments, accompanied by an orchestra.

country music a genre of popular music originating in the American rural south, with roots in European traditional music and the blues.

D

dB (decibel) a mathematical term used to express the relative levels of two electrical voltages.

decay the natural decline in the amplitude of a sound over time.

digital a word used to describe data and signals that have been sampled such that they can be represented by zeros and ones on a computer.

digital audio sound that has been sampled so that it can be manipulated in a computer or other device with the capacity to read it.

disco a genre of music that was popular in the 70's. It was characterized by an ostinato dance beat and repetitive lyrics.

dissonance a non-harmonic, clashing chord or note in relation to another note or chord that is not pleasing to the ear.

dominant (1) the fifth degree of the diatonic scale; (2) the triad or seventh chord built on this degree, having the quality of leading to the tonic; (3) the key oriented around this degree.

doowop a genre of music popular in the 1950s, with four to five voices singing in close harmony.

double (1) have the ability to play more than one instrument; (2) alternate playing two or more instruments in the same session or performance. Union players who double on a session are paid more for doing so.

double stop (also: triple, quadruple) on stringed instruments, the sounding of two or more notes (using two or more strings) at once.

downbeat the strong beat, normally the first beat of a measure.

duet a musical piece or section performed by two people.

duple meter the grouping of beats of measure into twos, a strong beat and a weak beat.

dynamics variations of volume with in a musical work.

E

electronic music a genre wherein most or all of the sounds are created by synthesizers.

ensemble (1) a group of musical performers;

(2) a passage in music where all performers are playing together.

exposition the first section of a movement in sonata form.

expression (1) the character of a musical work; (2) the feeling brought to a performance by a performer.

F

fermata a musical symbol indicating that a note or rest is to be held beyond its normal value.

finale (fi-NAL-ee) the ending movement or song of a large musical work.

fingerboard the wood that extends from the body of a string instrument; the strings are attached from the body to the end of the fingerboard.

flat (1) in musical notation, a symbol placed before a note indicating that the note is to be played a half step lower; (2) a term used to specify a specific note, e.g., B flat. (3) also used as an adjective to describe a note or player that is off key by playing or singing slightly too low.

folk music (1) music that originates from the common people of a nation or region and is passed from generation to generation orally. (2) music written in a traditional style, usually played on acoustic instruments.

form standardized order of certain sections; e.g., AABA song form or sonata allegro form.

forte; fortissimo loud; very loud

frequency indication of how many cycles of a repetitive waveform occur in 1 second. A waveform which has a repetition cycle of once per second has a frequency of 1Hz (pronounced Hertz).

frequency response a measurement of the frequency range that can be handled by a specific piece of electrical equipment or loudspeaker.

fundamental the basic pitch of a tone.

funk a style of popular dance music combining elements of jazz, blues and soul and characterized by syncopated rhythm and a heavy, repetitive bass line.

FX short for Effects.

G

gamelan a small Javanese orchestra consisting mainly of metal percussion instruments.

gangsta rap a form of rap music characterized by violent, often degrading lyrics.

genre a category of music. Songs or pieces are said to be of the same genre if they share similar form, instrumentation, subject matter and/ or style.

glissando a rapid sliding from one note to another, usually on continuous-pitch instruments such as the trombone or violin, but also on discrete-pitch instruments such as the piano or harp.

gospel music; gospel (1) a genre of music originating in American southern black church choirs with influences from protestant hymns and spirituals. Characterized by emotional vocals, harmony, melodic embellishment by soloist, and call-and-response between soloist and choir (2) contemporary music with Christian subject matter.

grunge a genre of non-flashy, non-technical rock originating in Seattle in the 1980's.

H

half step (semitone) the interval between any two adjacent notes on a keyboard; the smallest interval in common use in Western music.

harmonic any of the frequencies above the fundamental which are components of a complex waveform.

harmonic distortion the addition of harmonics that were not present in the original signal.

harmonica a small, hand-held reed instrument. Also known as "mouth organ," "Blues Harp," or "French harp," sometimes shortened to "harp."

harmonize to provide a melody with a chordal accompaniment.

harmony (1) the chords of a given piece of music; (2) the simultaneous playing of two or more different notes.

harpsichord a Baroque keyboard instrument in which the strings are plucked by quills.

head in jazz music, the original melody of a piece, usually played prior to improvised sections.

heavy metal a genre of rock music originating in the 1970s, characterized by heavily amplified electric guitars, loud vocals and dark themes.

hip hop the cultural context of rap music found in the urban style of dress, speech and art.

hymn a simple religious song in several stanzas, sung in a church service by the congregation.

Hz short for Hertz, the unit of frequency.

I

imitation the successive repetition of a single musical idea in different voices.

improvisation; improv (2) the creation of music as it is being performed; (2) music, especially melody, created in this way. Jazz musicians are often valued for their skill at improvisation.

interpretation the manner in which a performer carries out a composer's performance directions.

interval the acoustical distance between two

pitches, reckoned by the number of intervening scale degrees.

introduction a passage or section that prepares the way for a more extended section.

inversion (1) an interval or chord with the same notes as another, but with notes in reversed or rotated positions, e.g., a C major triad is played c-e-g in root position; its first inversion is e-g-c; (2) the playing of a melody "upside down," i.e., with upward intervals played downwards and vice versa.

J

jargon specialized words associated with a particular field or industry, used mainly or exclusively by those in that industry.

jazz American music born in the early 20th century, derived from African rhythms and slave chants, and Euro-American forms and instrumentation. In its short history, jazz has changed and branched often, and has defied musical definition. It is strongly associated with improvisation, sophisticated harmony, and syncopation.

K

k an abbreviation for 1000 (kilo). Used as a prefix to other values to indicate magnitude, as kHz (kilohertz).

key (1) in tonal music, one of twelve possible tonalities organized around a triad built on the main note. (2) on a keyboard instrument, a lever pressed down to produce sound.

key signature sharps or flats placed at the beginning of a staff to indicate the key of a passage or work.

keyboard (1) a set of keys arranged on instruments such as piano or organ.

(2) a synthesizer or midi controller with keys arranged as a piano or organ's.

L

Latin music a very broad category encompassing many genres of music having origins in South and Central America, Mexico and much of the Caribbean, and by extension, Africa. Tango, samba, bossa nova, meringue, salsa, and mariachi are a few of many internationally-appreciated Latin genres.

legato playing style where successive notes are smoothly, seamlessly connected.

libretto (Italian for "little book") the words of an opera or other long vocal work.

M

major (1) **scale** seven (ascending) notes in a particular pattern of whole and half steps (W, W, h, W, W, W, h) (2) **mode** the feeling of tone center based on this scale, generally sounding bright and stable; (3) **triad** a three-note chord consisting of a major third with a minor third stacked on top, bounded by a perfect fifth.

march a military style or piece characterized by strongly accented duple meter and clear sectional structures.

mass (1) the central worship service of the Roman Catholic Church; (2) the music written for that service.

melisma; melismatic (meh-LIZ-mah; mel-iz-MAT-ic) the technique of singing in which a single syllable is sung over two or more notes.

melody (1) a succession of single notes in a coherent arrangement; (2) a particular succession of such notes (also referred to as tune, theme, or voice).

medium the intervening substance, such as water or air, through a force acts on objects. Plural: media.

meter a grouping of pulses with a regular accent pattern, also called the "time" of the music.

metronome marking a number, usually placed at the top of a piece, that indicates tempo by telling how many beats of a certain note value will be heard per minute, for example, quarter note = 60.

metronome a mechanical or electrical device that ticks and/or blinks out a regular pulse. Can tick at 40 to 208 beats per minute.

mezzo (MET-zoh) medium, as in mezzo-piano (medium soft).

microtones intervals smaller than a half step.

MIDI acronym for Musical Instrument Digital Interface. A standard set of numeric commands to enable keyboards and other electronic musical devices to "talk" to each other, regardless of manufacturer. MIDI commands can be used to program and control notes, volume, vibrato, and hundreds of other parameters.

minor (1) **scale** seven ascending notes in a particular pattern of whole and half steps. There are three common minor scales: natural (W, h, W, W, h, W, W), harmonic, and melodic; (2) **mode** the feeling of tone center based on this scale, generally darker and more unstable than major; (3) **triad** a three-note chord consisting of a minor third with a major third stacked on top, bounded by a perfect fifth.

minuet a seventeenth-century court dance in moderate triple meter that later served as the model for the third movement of Classical instrumental works.

mode (1) in the tonal system, one of the two colorings, called major and minor, that may be applied to any of twelve keys, (2) loosely speaking, any scale, differentiated based on the order of whole and half steps, on which melody and harmony can be based.

modulation the process of changing keys in a tonal work, as in "the modulation from C major to F minor."

monophonic one note at a time.

motet one of several varieties of polyphonic vocal music, mostly sacred, from the Middle Ages to the present.

motive; motif the smallest coherent unit of melody, usually as part of a larger musical idea.

movement a self-contained, independent portion of a larger piece, such as a symphony or concerto.

music broadly speaking, sounds organized to express a wide variety of human emotions.

musicology the scholarly study of music and its historical contexts.

musical theater; musical (1) theatrical presentation incorporating songs into the plot. (2) genre of songs written for musical theatre, often called show tunes or Broadway tunes. From the late 19th to the early 20th century, most popular songs, including many that became jazz standards, were written for musicals.

mute (1) a device used with brass or string instruments to muffle the tone. (2) a button on mixer (real or virtual) that silences a particular track.

N

natural (1) in musical notation, a sign indicating that the preceding accidental applied to this note is to be cancelled; (2) the name given to such a note, for example, C natural.

New Age music modern music characterized quiet, soothing, sometimes dreamy repetitive melody, often involving a simple palette of sounds.

nocturne ("night piece") a piece of music that suggests night time. Most often used to describe short piano pieces.

non-legato the slight separation of adjacent notes.

notation a word used to describe the way music is written. Most MIDI programs can show and print MIDI notes as regular music notation.

note (1) a sound with a specific pitch and duration; (2) in musical notation, the symbol representing such a sound; (3) the letter name for a pitch (e.g. F#).

O

octave the interval in which one pitch is doubled (or halved) in frequency by another pitch. The octave is found in virtually all music systems.

odd meter meter in which the number of beats per measure cannot be divided by two or three.

opera a drama set to music, wherein vocal music in integral and central to the theatrical performance.

operetta a version of Romantic opera with lighter style and subject matter.

opus a "work"; opus numbers were introduced by publishers in the seventeenth century to identify each of a composer's works.

oratorio a musical work, usually on a sacred subject; unlike opera, an oratorio is generally performed in concert, without costumes or action, though it may include dramatic narrative.

orchestra an ensemble of varied instruments, often including strings, woodwinds, brass and percussion. The size of an orchestra varies according to the works it is to perform and the venue where it will perform. Symphony orchestras are large ensembles consisting of around 90 players. Chamber orchestras can have from 15 to 50 players. Theater orchestra vary widely. In order to execute a performance an orchestra normally needs a conductor.

orchestration the designation of what instruments are to play what voices or notes in a composition. The process of orchestrating is often referred to as scoring.

organ an instrument in which air forced through pipes by mechanical means is controlled by one or more keyboards, including a foot-operated pedal keyboard.

ornament an embellishment, such as a trill, used to decorate a melodic line.

ostinato a brief melody or rhythmic pattern repeated over and over again, often in the bass.

overtones the spectrum of the higher-pitched frequencies that accompany the fundamental of any pitch and determine its tone color (also called harmonics or partials).

overture an instrumental piece written as an opening to a dramatic work such as an opera (some overtures are nevertheless independent compositions).

P

part (1) one of the voices in a polyphonic work; (2) the written music for a single player or section in an ensemble.

pedal point long-held tones, most often in the bass or low register.

pentatonic scale a five-note scale, usually with no half-steps, found in numerous non-Western musics and adopted as an exotic element by many twentieth-century Western composers. It is easy to play pentatonic music using only the black keys on a piano

percussion instruments, either pitched or non-pitched, that produce sounds by being struck, rattled, or scraped. Common percussion include drums, cymbals, and bells.

performance directions words or symbols provided by composers to instruct performers in how their music is to be played, including articulation, dynamics, and expression.

phrasing the manner in which a performer organizes and presents the parts of a composition.

piano a keyboard instrument whose tone is produced by hammers striking strings tightly stretched over a large soundboard. A foot pedal controls the damping of the strings.

piano; pianissimo soft; very soft.

piano trio a chamber work for piano and two other instruments, usually violin and cello.

pitch (1) the high and low of sounds, measured in acoustical frequencies; (2) a particular note, such as middle C. (3) musical interpretation of an audio frequency, named by letters, A, B, C, etc.

pizzicato the technique of playing a string instrument that is normally bowed by plucking the strings with the finger.

plainchant (plainsong, Gregorian chant) monophonic unison music sung during Catholic church services since the Middle Ages.

polyphony the ability of an instrument to play two or more notes simultaneously. An instrument which can only play one note at a time is described as monophonic.

polyphonic (poly-fon-ick) a musical texture in which two or more individual voices (i.e., parts, instrumental or vocal) move independently of one another.

polyrhythm a texture in which the rhythms of various voices seem to exist independently of one another.

pop (1) a generic term for popular music in contemporary America; (2) Top 40 music, as distinguished from R&B, rock or other genres.

portamento a gliding effect that allows a sound to change pitch at a gradual rate, rather than abruptly, when a new key is pressed or MIDI note sent.

post production (1) work done to a stereo recording after mixing is complete; (2) phase in filmmaking or game production in which the musical score and sound effects are created and added to the visuals.

prelude a piece of music introducing another piece (though Chopin and other nineteenth-century composers wrote preludes that stood as independent works).

premier the first public performance of a musical or dramatic work.

prepared piano in contemporary music, the modifying of a traditional grand piano by such techniques as placing various objects between the strings.

presto; prestissimo very fast; extremely fast.

program music an instrumental work associated explicitly by the composer with a story or other extramusical idea.

progression see chord progression

punk a subgenre of rock music originating in the 1970s characterized by loud, aggressive, non-technical performance and anti-establishment, often deliberately offensive lyrics.

Q

quarter tone an interval equal to half a semitone, not commonly used in Western music

quartet (1) a piece for four singers or instrumentalists; (2) a group of four singers or instrumentalists.

quintet (1) A piece for five singers or instrumentalists; (2) a group of five singers or instrumentalists.

R

raga a traditional form in Hindu music, improvised within a framework of progressions, melodic formulas and rhythmic patterns.

ragtime a style of jazz, often for piano, with elaborately syncopated rhythm in the melody and a steadily accented accompaniment.

range the pitch distance between the lowest note and the highest note of an instrument, a composition, or an individual part.

rap genre of popular music of American black origin that features rapidly and rhythmically spoken lyrics over a background of repetitive electronic or sampled sounds, often featuring rhythmically scratched records as an instrument.

recapitulation the third principal section of a movement in sonata form whose function is to resolve the harmonic conflicts set up in the exposition and development.

recitative a flexible, often rubato style of vocal delivery employed in opera, oratorio, and cantata and tailored to the accents and rhythms of the text.

reed in wind instruments such as the clarinet and oboe, a small vibrating element made of cane that serves as all (double reed) or part (single reed) of the mouthpiece.

reeds collectively, all the instruments that have a vibrating reed or reeds

reggae a genre of popular music of Jamaican origin having elements of Calypso, soul and rock and characterized by an accentuated offbeat.

register the relative location within the range of a voice or an instrument, such as *the upper register of the oboe.*

release the rate at which a signal amplitude decays once a key has been released.

rest (1) in music, a brief silence; (2) in musical notation, a sign indicating such a silence.

retransition in sonata form, the passage that leads from the harmonic instability of the development to the stability of the recapitulation.

retrograde the composition technique of playing a melodic motive or theme backward.

rhythm & blues (R&B) a genre of music of American black origin, with roots in gospel and blues, and jazz rhythms. This term, coined in 1949 to describe the heavily rhythmic dance music, was eventually used to describe all popular music made by black musicians for a predominantly black audience; it of course spread to a larger audience. This genre influenced all popular music that came after it, and is one of the "parent" genres of rock.

rhythm (1) the pattern in time created by the incidence and duration of individual sounds; (2) used more loosely to refer to a particular rhythm, for example, "a dotted rhythm."

ritard; ritardando slowing down the tempo.

rock perhaps the most successful genre of 20th century popular music, a combination of R&B and country, with strong roots in blues and folk. It has developed since the early 1950s into numerous subgenres, and has influenced all popular music that came after it.

rondo a musical form in which a main theme alternates with other themes or sections, for example, A-B-A-C-A, etc.

round a simple sung canon in which all voices enter on the same note after the same time interval.

rubato (Italian, "Robbed" time); the subtle pressing forward and holding back of the tempo in performance.

S

salsa a popular form of Latin American dance music, characterized by AfroCaribbean rhythms, Cuban big band dance melodies and elements of jazz and rock.

scale an array of fixed, ordered pitches bounded by two notes an octave apart. The common Western scales contain seven notes.

scherzo (Italian, "joke") a faster, often humorous movement, a transformation of a minuet, introduced into symphonies by Beethoven.

score the complete musical notation of a composition, especially for an ensemble; the individual parts are lined up vertically.

scoring the process of orchestration.

section (1) a passage of a song or other piece of music that can be heard as a distinct unit within the whole; (2) a group of musicians in a band or orchestra playing the same instrument or family of instruments, e.g., *the cello section*, or *the horn section*.

semitone see halfstep.

sequence (1) any arrangement in which things follow a particular order or pattern (2) the repetition of a musical idea at progressively higher or lower pitches; (3) common short term for MIDI sequence, a list of MIDI-coded instructions (notes, durations, volume and pan controllers, etc) to a synthesizer. These instructions are found in a track or set of tracks in a file. To "sequence" is to create such tracks in a computer program or device.

shape the interrelationship through time of the parts or sections of a piece. Standardized shapes are commonly referred to as forms.

sharp in musical notation, a sign (#) indicating that the note it precedes is to be played a half step higher.

simple meter a meter in which the main beats are subdivided into twos.

sine wave the waveform of a pure tone with no harmonics.

ska a genre of popular music originating in Jamaica, characterized by fast rhythms emphasizing the off beat. Ska was a forerunner to reggae.

slur (1) in musical notation, a curved line connecting notes that are to be played legato; (2) in performance, the playing of legato.

SMPTE time code; SMPTE (SIMP-tee) A standard that allows audio and video (or other) devices to be synchronized precisely. The code is recorded or "striped" to film, video or audio synchronization reference. The invention of SMPTE code was a significant innovation in motion picture and television editing.

sonata a chamber work in several movements

sonata form a musical form or style, originating in the eighteenth century, based on successive stages of stability, tension, and resolution; the most influential form developed during the age of tonality.

song cycle a collection of poems set to music and tied together by mood or story line.

sonority a general term for sound quality, either of a brief moment or of an entire composition.

soprano (1) the high woman's (or boy's) voice; (2) the highest voice in a polyphonic texture.

soul a sub-genre of rhythm and blues built on elements of gospel and spiritual music, but with secular subject matter. Often, practitioners such as Sam Cooke maintained two careers simultaneously in soul and popular music.

staccato (1) a playing style where adjacent

notes are detached, short, crisp. (2) musical notation instructing the player to play in this way, indicated by a dot placed above a note head.

staff (plural, staves) in musical notation, the five horizontal lines on which one or more voices are notated.

stem in musical notation, the vertical line attached to a note head.

stereo a two-channel system feeding left and right loudspeakers.

stop on the organ, hand-operated levers that activate different means of sound production, thereby varying the tone color and volume of notes.

string quartet (1) ensemble consisting of two violins, viola, and cello; (2) a work composed for this ensemble.

style the result of the interaction among rhythm, melody, harmony, texture, color, and shape that make the music of a particular period or composer its distinctive.

subdominant (1) the fourth degree of the diatonic scale (2) the triad built on this degree; (3) the key oriented around this degree.

subject (1) what lyrics are written about (2) main theme of a fugue.

suite (1) a work consisting of a collection of dances, popular in the Baroque; (2) an abbreviated version of a longer work, for example, the suite from the film Star Wars.

swing (1) a style of jazz playing whose flexible, improvised rhythms resist notation; (2) name used to describe big band jazz from the 1930s and 1940s.

symphonic poem see Tone Poem.

symphony a large orchestral composition in several movements; a dominant form of public music in the eighteenth and nineteenth centuries.

sync short for synchronization; a system for making two or more pieces of equipment run at exactly the same time, at the same rate.

syncopation the accenting, within a well-defined meter, of weaker beats or portions of beats.

synthesizer an electronic musical instrument designed to create a wide range of sounds, both imitative and abstract.

system group of staves connected by a vertical line, indicating that they are to be played simultaneously.

T

tail the end of a theme.

tango a duple-meter dance from Argentina that was popular in Paris in the early twentieth century.

tempo (Italian, "time") the speed of a piece of music, usually reckoned by the rate of beats per minute.

tenor (1) the high male voice; (2) the second-lowest voice in a four-part texture; (3) the second-lowest instrument in the saxophone family.

ternary form a three-part musical structure (ABA) based on statement (A), contrast (B), and repetition (A).

texture the musical weave of a composition, such as homophonic or contrapuntal.

thematic anticipation the practice of introducing fragments of a theme before presenting it in its entirety, originating in the Romantic period.

theme a self-contained melodic idea from which larger musical works are developed.

theme and variations popular form in which a theme is followed by variations that preserve the phrase lengths and harmonization of the theme while varying its rhythms, melodies, and textures.

timbre the tonal 'color' of a sound.

time signature the two numbers that appear in a score immediately after the key signature. The upper number indicates how many beats each measure is to receive; the lower number indicates the value of the note that receives each beat.

tonality; tonal   a harmonic system in which triads are arranged hierarchically around a central triad called the tonic. In this system, the tonic has a feeling of "home," or "rest."

tone   (1) a general term for pitch or note; (2) the sound quality or character of a given pitch; timbre.

tone duster   the simultaneous sounding of adjacent pitches.

tone color (timbre)   the acoustical properties of a sound, including its envelope and the distribution of overtones above the fundamental.

tone poem (symphonic poem)   a piece of orchestral program music in one long movement.

tone row   in serial music, the ordering of all twelve notes of the chromatic scale to serve as the basis of a composition.

tonic   (1) the first degree, or central note, of the diatonic scale; (2) the triad built on this degree; (3) the key oriented around this degree.

transcription   (1) the written or printed version of a particular recorded piece of music or part. In order to study his craft, a musician may *transcribe*, i.e., write out every note of, the arrangement or solo of another great musician; (2) an arrangement, usually for a solo instrument such as a piano, of an orchestral or vocal work.

transducer   a device for converting one form of energy to another. A microphone is a good example of a transducer as it converts mechanical energy to electrical energy.

transition   (1) any musical passage with a feeling of instability or other technique leading the ear to another passage; (2) in a movement in sonata form, the unstable stage in an exposition that undertakes the modulation from the tonic to the new key.

transpose   to move a passage (or section or entire work) from one pitch level to another.

treble clef   the clef in the upper staff that denotes pitches mostly above middle C.

tremolo   in string playing, repetitions of a tone produced by rapid alternation between up-and-down strokes of the bow.

triad   a chord consisting of three pitches constructed around intervals of interlocking thirds (on the white notes, this amounts to every other note).

trill   a musical ornament that consists of two notes a half step or a whole step apart played in rapid alternation.

trio   (1) a work for three performers; (2) the second section of a Baroque dance such as a minuet.

triple meter   the regular grouping of beats into threes, as in a waltz.

triplet   the grouping of three notes played evenly in the same amount of time as two notes of usual duration. Triplets are notated by a bracket with a number 3 over the three notes of a particular duration. Thus, three bracketed quarter notes are played in the same amount of time that two quarter notes would ordinarily take.

tritone   an interval of an augmented fourth or diminished fifth, consisting of three whole step. This very dissonant interval was known in medieval music as "the devil in music."

tune   (1) to adjust the pitch of a note or instrument to a particular frequency; (2) an informal term for a melody; (3) industry slang for a song or record.

tutti   (Italian, "all") the full ensemble, usually written after a solo, duet or similar section to say, "now everyone play."

U

unison   a descriptive term for music sung or played at the same pitch by two different voices or instruments.

upbeat   a weak or unaccented beat that anticipates a strong downbeat.

V

variation   (1) generally, an altered version of a rhythm, motive, or theme; (2) in theme and variations, each regular section following the theme, in which the phrase lengths and harmonization remain true (or close) to the theme while the rhythms, melodies, and textures change.

verse   (1) a stand-alone song section. (2) in AABA "standards," term sometimes given to the introductory verse, a section prior to the AABA form.

vibrato   small but rapid fluctuations in pitch, especially in the human voice or on a violin instrument.

virtuosity   in a composition, a focus on exceptional technical demands; in a performance, a focus on exceptional technical display.

virtuoso   a performer with exceptional technical skills.

voice   (1) the human voice; (2) an independent line in any polyphonic piece.

W

wah pedal   a guitar effects device where a bandpass filter is varied in frequency by means of a pedal control.

walking bass   a playing or composition style in which a bass part moves steadily in constant rhythms.

waltz   (1) a song or piece in triple meter; (2) a dance in moderate to fast triple meter.

warmth   a subjective term used to describe sound where the bass and low mid frequencies have depth and where the high frequencies are smooth sounding rather than being aggressive or fatiguing. "Warm-sounding" tube equipment may also produce some of the effects as compression.

waveform   a graphic representation of the way in which a sound wave or electrical wave varies with time.

whole step (whole tone)   an interval equal to two half steps.

whole-tone scale   a scale of only whole tones (whole steps), having six steps in an octave. Since it removes the traditional sense of tonality, it is not commonly used in western music. However, Debussy and other western composers experimented with its use.

wind instrument   any instrument which makes a sound by forcing air through it, as brass, woodwinds, or organs.

woodwinds   a family of instruments, constructed largely of wood, that produce sound by means of blowing air across an aperture or through a vibrating reed.

Z

zydeco   a genre of music out of Louisiana's bayous that blends French Cajun rhythms with rhythm and blues, rock and country. Instrumentation traditionally includes washboards and accordions, though electric guitar, bass and drums are now also used.

Appendix A: Setting Up Your Score For Recording

The score should be spiral bound or connected in such a way that the music lies flat on a table or music stand when opening. Any music made for a musician should be in ink, either from a pen or computer printer. Pencil should not be used because it can be too faint, can smudge, and can reflect light, all of which make it hard to read.

Setting Up your music for a recording

Setting Up a Score

No matter what form the music takes, everyone involved must understand it and be able to follow it. That's what's most important.

1. If your measures are not numbered you should first number each measure. You can number them at the beginning of the measure or in the middle of the measure. Do not position numbers at the ends of measures (see A.130).

When using Midi or digital numbering – i.e., SMPTE time code – or minutes and seconds, the repeat of a section is considered new material and not a repeat of previous music. When you have a repeat sign, D.S. or D.C. you should continue numbering the measures as if all measures of the repeated section were written out. This means you will have two sets of numbers for some measures, and the numbers will be continued after the repeat sign (see A.131 and A.132).

2. Use rehearsal letters to identify sections in the song. SMPTE time or minutes and seconds should be added to the score at each rehearsal letter and at distinctive musical points in the score if SMPTE code is being used. Again, this may mean you have two sets of numbers at some rehearsal letters.

3. You may wish to highlight repeats, D.S. & Coda markings. Some people put a tab or paperclip anywhere they may have to turn pages back or forward quickly.

4. The score should be bound such that it lays flat on a table or music stand when opened. Spiral or comb binding works well. In addition to the conductor's score, there should be a score for the engineer and a score for the producer.

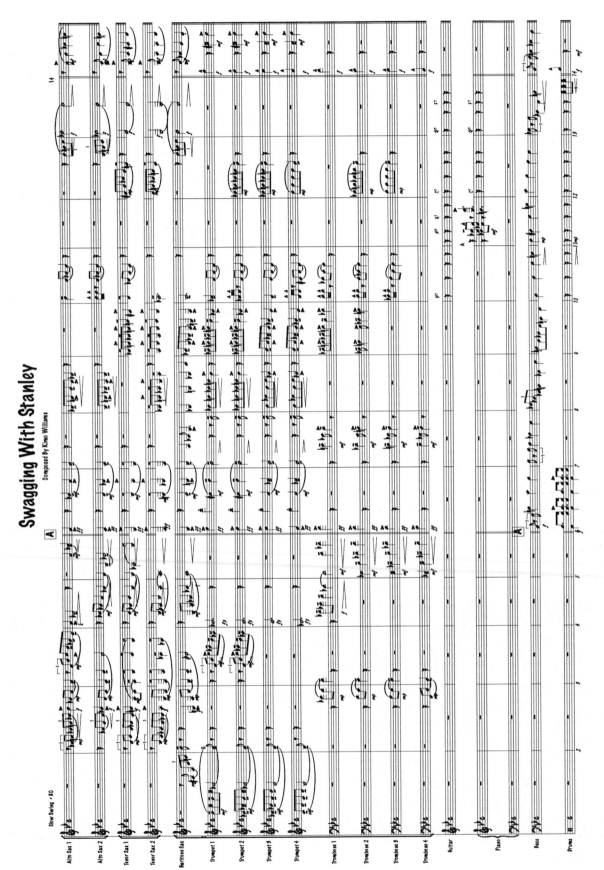

Figure A.130

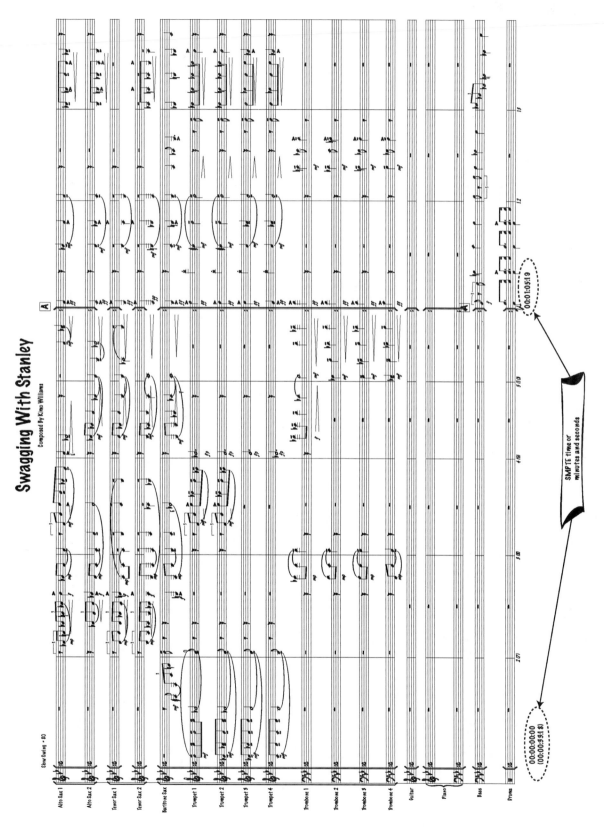

Figure A.131

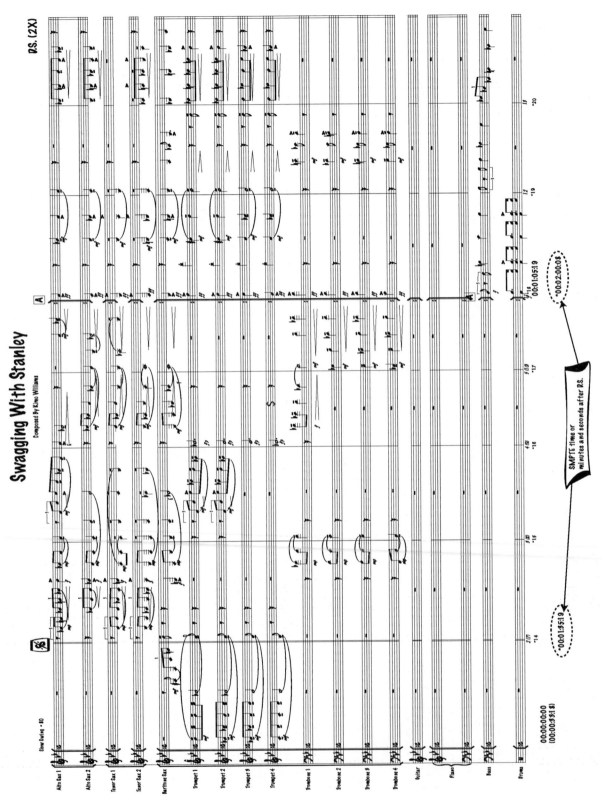

Figure A.132

Setting Up Chord Charts

Chord charts can be used for all participants in smaller sessions, in place of a leadsheet. A chord chart is a simple rendering of the music, with chords and minimum of information. Most are on one page, sometimes two. They are common for rhythm section recordings. They are best printed on heavy paper in dark ink. If hand written, write neatly and large enough so that all instructions can be read quickly; remember, this will be read in real time as the music is being played. Unless the piece is very long, rehearsal letters are not used on a chord chart.

- Write out measure numbers.
- Make sure chord symbols are correct and legible.
- Each measure should have slash marks, one for each beat, wherever musicians are expected to play. 1- and 2-bar repeat signs are common.
- If a specific rhythm is required, large rhythmic notation indicates that all players hit the same rhythms simultaneously. This can include silences, which are marked with rests.
- Mark repeats, if any.

Chord Charts with Lyrics

In some cases only the lyrics and chords are used to follow the music. These can be set up as chord charts, with slashes and other directions. The beats should be indicated with slashes and measures should be identified; repeats, if any should be clearly marked (fig. A.133a&b). Occasionally the staves are not used and only the barlines show (figs. A.134a&b).

Practice

Figure A.135a-w is a 24-page score to use for practice. Look over the score then follow along with Track 95.

To help keep your place in the music, it may help to mark or highlight certain events in the score.

1. Places where instruments are entering for a particular section.

2. Measure numbers

3. Locations of tempo change, as, of course, it will affect counting.

Count along and practice following in the music while listening. It may take several times through before you feel confident that you are in the right place in the music at the same time as the instruments.

Next try following the line for only one instrument. Focus on listening to just that particular instrument's part while counting.

© 1986 by Little Beck Music

Figure A.133a: Leadsheet, page 1

Figure A.133b: Leadsheet, page 2

© 1986 by Little Beck Music

Figure A.134a: Chord chart made from preceding pages' leadsheet, page 1

Figure A.134b: Chord chart made from preceding pages' leadsheet, page 2

Track 95 - Symphony For The Sons of Nam Chapter 2 - James Kimo Williams

Figure A.136a: Practice score, page 1

Figure A.136a: Practice score, page 2

Figure A.136a: Practice score, page 3

Figure A.136a: Practice score, page 4

Figure A.136a: Practice score, page 5

Figure A.136a: Practice score, page 6

Figure A.136a: Practice score, page 7

Figure A.136a: Practice score, page 8

Figure A.136a: Practice score, page 9

Figure A.136a: Practice score, page 10

Figure A.136a: Practice score, page 11

Figure A.136a: Practice score, page 12

Figure A.136a: Practice score, page 13

Figure A.136a: Practice score, page 14

Figure A.136a: Practice score, page 15

Figure A.136a: Practice score, page 16

Figure A.136a: Practice score, page 17

Figure A.136a: Practice score, page 18

Figure A.136a: Practice score, page 19

Figure A.136a: Practice score, page 20

Figure A.136a: Practice score, page 21

Figure A.136a: Practice score, page 22

Figure A.136a: Practice score, page 23

Figure A.136a: Practice score, page 24

Appendix B – Answers to Practical Exercises

Lesson 1 Answers

A. Questions
1. Group or individual who perform(s) music, and whose name goes on a recording
2. Reading music is seeing and understanding musical symbols. Sight-reading is playing or singing music while reading it, in real time, without stopping for mistakes.
3. Improvising is making up a melody or lead part; comping is making up a stylistically appropriate accompaniment.
4. A song is words and melody together. A Record is a particular recorded version of that song.
5. The musical decisions made for the performance or recording of a particular work or the written notation for all parts of the work
6,7. Sub-genre, method or pattern of playing, individual characteristic sound of a musician or writer
8, 9. Little or no harmonic content in accompaniment. Melodic line is secondary to lyric and groove.
10. Blues, folk, gospel, spirituals, hymns, bluegrass, "world"

B. Matching
1. l, n, o
2. a, c, f, k
3. h
4. j
5. d, i, g, (b)
6. b
7. e, p
8. m, (g)

Lesson 2 Answers

A. Questions
1. By the type and order of sections
2. Verse-Chorus
3. A short piece of music, repeated until cued to continue or stop
4. In an AABA song, the bridge is the B section.
5. A refrain is one line which is a part of a verse (usually at the beginning or end of the verse). A chorus is a section separate from the verse.
6. AABA
7. (a) An opening section that is not repeated, different from the rest of the song. (b) common in AABA

Lesson 3 Answers

A. Questions
1. Preserved through memorization and passed down orally.
2. Easy to write, uses less ink, allows interpretation by the performer(s)
3. More precise. Writer can get exactly what he/she wants.
4. 5
5. Whole note
6. Eighth note
7. A beam connects a group of eighth notes.
8. The left side.
9. Sheet music (def. b) has a written piano accompaniment; lead sheets do not.

B. Visual Practice
1. 4
2. 2
3. 1
4. 1 ½
5. 4

6. 3
7. 7
8. 3
9. 3
10. 4 ½

Lesson 4 Answers

A. Questions

1. The speed of music at which music is played

2. A grouping of pulses that repeats and serves as the rhythmic 'framework' for music.

3. 4/4

B. Visual Practice

1. 3/4
2. 4/4
3. 3/4
4. 6/8
5. 3/4
6. 6/4
7. 4/4
8. 3/4
9. 3/4 or 6/8
10. 4/4

Lesson 6 Answers

A. Questions

1. A sound wave requires an ear to interpret it for the brain to consider it a sound.

2. Transducers change acoustical energy into electrical impulses, or vice-verse. An organic transducer is the cochlea.

3. Temporary Threshold Shift

4. Attack, Decay, Sustain, Release

5. Decibels Sound Pressure Level

6. 0-220 dB SPL

7. Frequency, wavelength, amplitude

8. Hz, inches/feet, dB SPL

9. Pitch, volume, timbre

10. Amplitude corresponds to volume. Frequency and wavelength correspond to pitch.

11. Overtones. Higher frequencies that sound above and in addition to the fundamental (lowest) pitch.

12. Timbre

Lesson 7 Answers

A. Questions

1. It assigns a pitch to each line and space; without it, a musician won't know which pitches to play.

2. Short, "extended" staff lines used when a note falls outside the range of the staff; drawn only when needed.

3. Treble/G clef 𝄞 , Alto or Tenor/C clef 𝄡 Bass/ F clef 𝄢 Percussion clef ‖ or ▯

4. C Clef

5. Sharp

6. Sharp ♯ – Raises the note after it a half step higher

Flat ♭ – Raises the note after it a half step lower

Natural ♮ – Returns a note to "normal" after a sharp or flat.

B. Visual Practice

7.

213

Lesson 7 Answers, B Visual Practice
(continued)

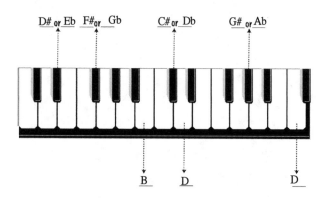

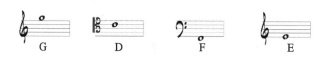

G   C   B   A

G   D   F   E

A   A   F   D

Lesson 8 Answers

A. Questions

1. By the number of half-steps and/or whole-steps between 2 notes.
2. Harmonic - sounded simultaneously, melodic – sounded in succession
3. Half-step or minor 2nd
4. Octave, fifth, fourth.
5. Second, third, sixth, seventh
6. A set of sharps or flats at the beginning of a piece that tells the performer to play these accidentals throughout the piece of music
7. F#
8. E b
9. Diminished
10. Minor
11. Augmented
12. Third, sixth, seventh

Lesson 8. B Visual Practical – 1

1.

2.

3.

4.

5.

6.

7.

8.

Lesson 8. B Visual Practice – 2

1. maj. 7th
2. aug. 4th/dim. 5th
3. min. 3rd
4. min. 7th
5. min. 3rd
6. P4
7. min. 6th
8. P

Lesson 8. B Visual Practice – 2

(continued)

9. maj. 3rd
10. min. 2nd
11. maj. 6th
12. maj. 3rd
13. P8ve
14. min. 6th
15. maj. 2nd
16. P5

B. Visual Practice – 3

1. major 7th

2. minor 7th

3. minor 3rd

4. diminished 4

5. minor 3rd

6. perfect 4th

7. minor 6th

8. perfect 4th

9. major 3rd

10. major 3rd

11. major 6th

12. major 3rd

13. perfect octave

14. perfect 5th

15. major 2nd

16. majo 6th

Lesson 8. B Visual Practice – 4

1. Cb
2. F#
3. Ab
4. B
5. C#
6. Gb
7. Eb
8. E
9. F
10. D
11. Db
12. Bb
13. G
14. A

Lesson 8. B Visual Practice – 5

1.
2.
3.
4.
5.
6.
7.
8.
9.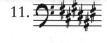
10.
11.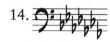
12.
13.
14.
15.

Lesson 8. B Visual Practice – 6

1. maj. 7th
2. min. 6th
3. min. 3rd
4. aug. 4th
5. min. 2nd
6. min. 3rd
7. maj. 3rd
8. dim. 4th
9. dim. 3rd
10. aug. 2nd
11. dim. 5th
12. P5
13. aug. 6th
14. dim. 5th
15. maj. 7th
16. min. 2nd

Lesson 9 Answers

A. Questions

1. Notes played in addition to and as support for the melody.
2. Three notes played at once.
3. Major, minor, augmented, diminished, sustained.
4. Root, 3rd, 5th
5. Maj. 3rd, P5
6. Min. 3rd, P5
7. F is the root of the chord; Maj is the quality (of the triad) of the chord.

B. Visual Practice

1. B-flat seven
2. E minor
3. A-sharp diminished seven
4. D major
5. G major seven
6. C minor seven
7. F-sharp augmented

Lesson 9 Answers, Visual Practice-
(continued)
8.   B-flat diminished
9.   E seven sharp nine
10. A minor seven
11. D major seven
12. G-flat major
13. C minor seven flat five
14. F minor
15. B diminished
16. E augmented

Lesson 10 Answers

A. Questions
1.   Violin, piccolo, flute, soprano sax, trumpet, clarinet, soprano (singer)
2.   Viola, guitar, oboe, English horn, clarinet, alto/tenor sax, French horn, etc.
3.   Bassoon, contrabassoon, bass clarinet, baritone sax
4.   Trumpet(s), trombone(s), saxophone(s)
5.   Bass, drums, guitar, piano/keyboard
6.   Pizzicato, arco
7.   Kick, snare, hi-hat
8.   Ride
9.   Brass
10. Clarinets, saxophones
11. Soprano, Alto, Tenor, Bass
12. Arranger

B. Visual Practice
1.   French horn
2.   Synthesizer
3.   Shaker
4.   Bassoon
5.   Baritone sax
6.   Contrabass
7.   Snare drum
8.   Tubular bells
9.   Bongos
10. Oboe

C Audio Practice
1.   Tuba
2.   Soprano Sax
3.   Bassoon
4.   Trombone
5.   Marimba
6.   Cello
7.   Piccolo
8.   Baritone Sax
9.   Oboe
10. Synthesizer

Lesson 11 Answers

A. Questions
1.   Play very slowly
2   ♩ = 120
3.   Accelerando, ritardando
4.   Back to original tempo
5.   They are dynamic markings:
Forte: 𝆑 (play loudly)
Piano: 𝆏 (play softly)
6.   Play swing 8ths
7.   Articulations
8.   The guitar does not play
9.   Any member of the violin family might get the direction to (pizz.) pluck strings with the fingers, then (arco) resume using a bow.

Lesson 12 Answers

A. Questions
1.   Go back to the Segno (sign)
2.   Accent the note
3.   Go back to the beginning and play from through the Coda ending
4.   Large capital letters, often in a box, that identify sections. Crucial for efficient management of all involved in playing music together
5.   They are slash marks. Found in chord charts, they tell a rhythm section player to comp

B. Visual Practice
1.   c
2.   e
3.   f
4.   c
5.   d
6.   i
7   j
8.   a
9.   b
10. g

C. Score following
1.   meas. 10
2.   meas.9
3.   meas. 18
4.   meas. 23
5.   meas. 21
6.   meas. 83

Appendix C: Song List

Title	Artist /Writer	Year	Form	Meter	Sub-div of beat	Genre(s)
All Blue	Miles Davis	1960		3/4	Sw 8	J
Before He Cheats	Carrie Underwood/ Tompkins, Kear	2007	VC (B)	4/4	Sw 16	C, P
Big Yellow Taxi	Joni Mitchell, Various others/ Mitchell	1970	VC	4/4	16ths	Folk-R
Blue Christmas	various/ Hayes, Johnson	1948	ABAC	4/4	Sw 8	Blues, R
Blue Danube	Various/ Johann Strauss II	1903?		3/4	8ths	Classical
Capital G	Nine-Inch Nails/ Reznor	2007		12/8	8 trp (sw 8)	R
Clint Eastwood	Gorillaz/Gorillaz	2001	VC	4/4	8th	
Complicated	Avril Lavigne/ The Matrix	2002	I V R C	4/4	Sw 16	P, RB
Control	Janet Jackson/ Jackson, Harris, Lewis	1986	VC Br	4/4	8ths	RB/P
Could I Have This Dance	Anne Murray/Holyfield, House	1980	VC	3/4	8ths	C
Crazy	Gnarls Barkley/ Cee-lo, Danger Mouse	2006	VC	4/4	Str 8/ some 16th	P
Crazy Little Thing Called Love	Queen, Dwight Yokam (Gap Ad)/ Mercury	1980	VR Br	4/4	Sw 8	P R/C R
Do You Love Me	The Contours/ Gordy	1962	Ivr,	4/4	8 & Sw 8th	RB, Soul
Dreams	Fleetwood Mac	1977	VC	4/4	Str 8th	R
E-Pro	Beck/Beck	2005	VC w/Br	4/4	8ths & 16ths	Rp R
Every Little Thing She Does is Magic	Police	1981	VCw/Br	4/4	8th	R,P
Feel Good Inc	Gorillaz/ Gorillaz	2005		4/4	8th	
Friends in Low Places	Garth Brooks/ Lee, Blackwell	1990	VC	4/4	8th	C
Give It Away	Red Hot Chili Peppers	1991	VC w/Bdn		Sw 16th	Rp F-R
Hey Jude	Beatles	1968	AABA	4/4	begn: 8th; ends 16th	R
I Can Love You Like That	John Michael Montgomery, All-4-One/ Myers, Baker	1994	VC	4/4	8ths or 16ths	C/RB P
I Will Survive	Gloria Gaynor/ Perren, Fekaris	1978	VC	4/4	Str 8th	P
I'm a Believer	Various/ Diamond	1966	VC w/ Pr	4/4	8ths	P
I'm Your Baby Tonight	Whitney Houston	1990	VC	12/8	Trplts	
Killing Me Softly	Various/ Fox, Gimbel	1971	VC	4/4	8th	P
Longview	Green Day/ Dirnt, Armstrong	1994	VC	4/4	Sw 16, trpl	R
Lucy in the Sky with Diamonds	Beatles	1967	VC	12/8, 4/4	Trpl, Str 8th	R
Mama Said Knock you Out	LL Cool J	1990		4/4	Sw 16th	HH/Rp
Mambo No. 5 (A Little Bit of)	Lou Bega, others/ Prado	1949	VC	4/4	Sw 8	
Me Love	Sean Kingston/ Anderson (Bonham, Jones, Page, Plant)	2007	VC	4/4	16th	P, RB
Play That Funky Music	Wild Cherry/ Parissi	1976	VC w/Pr	4/4	Str 16th (subtle)	Disco, F
Pon De Replay (Radio Edit)	Rihanna/ Nobels, Sturkin, Rogers, Brooks	2005	V-R	4/4	Sw 8	J
Pretty Woman	Roy Orbison/ Orbison, Dees	1964	R-V w/Br	4/4	Str 8th	R
Purple Haze	Jimi Hendrix	1966	V-R	4/4	Str 8th	R
Rock Around the Clock	Bill Haley and His Comets	1954	VC	4/4	Swing 8th	R (RR)
Roll Over Beethoven	Chuck Berry/ Berrry	1956	V-R (or AABA)	4/4	Str 8th	R (RR)
Satisfaction	Rolling Stones/ Jaggers, Richards	1965		4/4	Straight 8th	R
Saving All My Love For You	Whitney Houston/ Masser, Goffin	1985/ '78	AABA	12/8	Trplts	P

Key to Abbreviations: **Out**=Outro, **(I)**=Introductory verse, **S**= solo instrumental or instrumental section **V**=Verse, **P** = Top 40, mainstream; **R**= Rock; **RR** = Rock & Roll, **RB** = R&B; **C** = Country, **F** = Funk, **J** = Jazz; **HH** = Hip Hop ; **Rp** = Rap; **L** = Latin; **Cls** = Classical

Title	Artist /Writer	Year	Form	Meter	Sub-div of beat	Genre(s)
Sexy and 17	Stray Cats	1985	VC	4/4	Swing 8th	RR
She Will Be Loved	Maroon 5/ Levine, Valentine	2002		4/4	Str 8	
So What	Miles Davis/ Davis	1959		4/4	Sw 8	J
So What You Want	Beastie Boys	1992	VC	4/4	Sw 16th	Rp/HH
Stand By Your Man	Tammy Wynette, Various others/ Sherrill, Wynette	1968	VC	4/4	Sw8th	C
Starting Over	John Lennon/Lennon	1980	VR IV B	12/8	(sw 8th)	
Superstition	Stevie Wonder / Wonder	1972		4/4	Sw 16	RB, F
Tutti Frutti	Little Richard/Penniman	1955	12B	4/4		R&R
Twilight Time	The Platters/Nevins,Nevins&Ram	1944	AABA	12/8		R
Vision of Love	Mariah Carey/Carey & Margulies	1990	V-R (or AABA)	12/8	Trplts	P
Where It's At	Beck/Beck	1996	VC	4/4	8th/16th	R
You Really Got Me	The Kinks/ Davies	1964	V-R	4/4	8ths	R

Accompanying Audio CD

The CD accompanying this book may be played on virtually any sound system as well as in your compuDer. You can also upload the tracks to your Ipod as the files are in the MP3 format and playable on both Mac computers and Windows Computers. The material on this CD is provided to reinforce specific lesson material and to use with audio excercises to test your understanding of the lessons. When you see the icon, ▦ you should press play on your CD player and locate the track number that is indicated next to the icon. During these lessons you should listen to the music passages recorded on the CD, following along with the written example.

Track	Page	Description
1	4	Classical Music
2	4	Two different styles of Jazz Music
3	7	Rap music example
4	7	Pop music example
5	30	Unaccented Metronome at 80 bpm
6	30	Unaccented Metronome at 60, 90, then 120 bpm
7	30	A continuous repeated pulse with specific emphasis pattern.
8	32	Figures 3.15 a & b, played as written
9	34	Each of the 3 melodies with count-off prior to playing and silence between
10	37	Duration: (a)whole note, (b)half note, (c)quarter note
11	38	Click, count-off, and counting 8th notes.
12	39	Counting 16th notes (with count-off)
13	41	Counting triplets (count off & click)
14	42	a: 8th note triplet, b: quarter note triplet, c: half note triplet, d: sixteenth note triplet
15	43	Three different rhythms (These rhythms as played, as in Fig 3.29)
16	44	Figure 3.32 a – d, as sung on Doo
17	45	Uniform, metrical rhythm
18	45	Syncopated rhythm accenting off beats
19	47	(a) 4 measures of straight 8th notes played on high-hat cymbals (b) 4 measures of a straight-8th rock drum groove
20	47	(a) 4 measures of swing 8th notes played on high-hat cymbals (b) 4 measures of a swing-8th drum groove
21	47	(a) 4 measures of straight 16th notes on high-hat cymbals (b) 4 measures of a straight-16th drum groove
22	47	(a) 4 measures of swing 16th notes on high-hat cymbals (b) 4 measures of a swing-16th drum groove
23	54	A 440, Concert A
24	54	A 880, one octave above Concert A
25	74	Two notes played (a) melodically, then (b) harmonically
26	75	Major scale ascending & descending

Track	Page	Description
27	75	Joy to the World
28	76	Fig. 5.70 as written: 8 consecutive steps on white keys, starting on D
29	76	D Major scale
30	77	an A minor scale
31	78	C major scale ascending & descending. C minor scale ascending & descending
32	102	Violin
33	102	Violin pizzicato
34	102	Violin played arco
35	102	Viola
36	102	Cello
37	102	Orchestra Strings playing legato
38	102	Orchestral Strings playing staccato
39	104	Nylon string acoustic guitar, strummed, then picked.
40	104	Steel string acoustic guitar, strummed, then picked.
41	104	Electric Guitar, strummed, then picked
42	104	Guitar with chorus effect
43	104	Guitar with distortion
44	104	Guitar with wah wah effect
45	104	Guitar with echo or delay
46	104	Electric Bass
47	105	Upright Bass
48	106	Harp
49	106	Piccolo
50	106	Flute
51	106	Oboe
52	106	English horn
53	108	Clarinet and Bass clarinet
54	108	Bassoon
55	108	Soprano sax
56	108	Alto saxophone
57	108	Tenor saxophone
58	108	Baritone saxophone
59	108	Harmonica
60	110	Trumpet
61	110	French Horn
62	110	Trombone
63	110	Tuba
64	112	Timpani
65	112	Xylophone
66	112	Marimba

Track	Page	Description
67	112	Vibraphone
68	112	Tubular Bells
69	114	Snare Drum
70	114	Bass Drum
71	114	Suspended cymbals
72	114	Triangle
73	114	Tambourine
74	114	Congas
75	114	Bongos
76	114	Shaker
77	117	Acoustic and electronic snares
78	117	Acoustic and electronic kick drums
79	117	Acoustic and electronic high hats
80	117	Tom toms
81	177	Ride cymbal with jazz rhythm
82	117	Crash and splash cymbals
83	117	Various drum sets and grooves
84	118	Piano
85	118	Electric Piano
86	118	Church Organ and Jazz organ
87	119	Synthesizers
88	126	Instrument I.D.s for practical exercises
89	150	Symphonic score-following practice exercise
90	151	Jazz score-follow practice exercise
91	152	Pop score-following practice exercise
92	153	Chamber music score-following practice exercise
93	155	3/4 time score-following practice exercise
94	156	Full-orchestra practice score exercise
95	188	Final practice score (*Symphony For The Sons of Nam, Chapter Two by* Kimo Williams

James "Kimo" Williams is an award-winning composer, musician, music business entrepreneur and educator. He was born in Amityville, New York, the son of a career Air Force serviceman. He spent much of his childhood on Air Force bases and on his grandparents' sharecropper farm in North Carolina. As a teenager he moved to Hawaii. Immediately after graduation from Leilehua High School he enlisted in the US Army. The night before enlisting he attended his first major concert – Jimi Hendrix at the Waikiki Bowl. Seeing Hendrix live inspired him to make music his life, and he dedicated himself to playing the guitar.

The day after his 20th birthday he was sent to Viet Nam, where he served with the 25th Combat Engineer Battalion in Lai Khe, building roads and clearing land in the jungle. An Army entertainment service director heard him playing guitar at a service club and suggested he form a soldier band to play for troops. He tour managed and music directed "The Soul Coordinators" who traveled to remote areas of South Vietnam, setting up their drums and amplifiers in the jungle mud. Their music often competed with artillery fire.

After leaving Viet Nam, he returned home to Hawaii and played in several Hawaii local rock bands. He then used his GI Bill benefit to attend the prestigious Berklee College of Music. Starting as a guitarist who could barely read music, he developed his composition talent and a unique writing style. Blending jazz, rock and classical elements, he created his own harmonic concepts (*Diagonal Harmony*) and formed the innovative Paumalu Symphony (now Kimotion), to play his compositions. After completing a BA in composition, he spent a year teaching at Berklee.

He re-enlisted into the Army Band program, went on to attend Officer Candidate School, and was commissioned a 2nd Lieutenant. Over the next several years, Kimo earned an MA in Management from Webster University. After reaching Captain he resigned from the Army to pursue composing full time and began his career as an educator. He taught various courses at Northeastern University in Chicago, Sherwood Conservatory of Music and at Columbia College Chicago, and was Bandmaster for the 85th Division Army Reserve Band.

Kimo's growing recording catalogue of his jazz influenced symphonic rock orchestra music featuring his orchestra "Kimotion", includes *War Stories* (1991), whose critical acclaim included 4 1/2 stars from Downbeat magazine. *Tracking* (2001) features friends Vinnie Colaiuta (formerly with Sting) on drums, Michael Brecker (tenor sax) and actor/musician Gary Sinise (CSI NY), on bass. He also released *Kimotion Live in 2004.* His full Symphonic Orchestra works include: *Symphony For the Sons of Nam, Fanfare For Life* commissioned by AT&T and *Buffalo Soldiers* commissioned by WestPoint. *Symphony For the Sons of Nam* has been Kimo Williams' most successful work. Several national and international groups, including the Savannah, Detroit, Philadelphia, Atlanta, Nashville and Indianapolis, Symphony Orchestras, have performed it. The score has been regularly programmed on NPR's *Performance Today*.

In 1999 Kimo was the 38th recipient of the Lancaster Symphony Composers Award, - for contributions to American Music.

In 2006 Kimo was selected as one of Chicago Magazines' Chicagoans of The Year and received a luncheon in his honor. In 2007 he was selected as a Fulbright Specialist to develop International programs in Jazz Improvisation.

Kimo has written five string quartets, and three symphonies and in 1997 composed the music for a Steppenwolf Theatre production of *A Streetcar Named Desire*, and music directed the 1997 Goodman Theatre's production of the August Wilson play, *Ma Rainey's Black Bottom*. As film composer he composed the score for *Arithmetic Lesson* a film by Tawaian film director Wenhwa Ts'ao.

In 1998 he created the *United States Viet Nam Arts Program* to produce collaborative artistic projects with Vietnam artists and American artists. He has returns to annually, working on this program and lecturing on American jazz for Vietnamese conservatories. In 2008 he took his 26 member Kimotion ensemble to Hue Vietnam to perform for their 2008 Festival of Arts.

Currently he is a tenured professor in the Music Business concentration in the Arts, Entertainment and Media Management Department at Columbia College in Chicago.

The Lt. Dan Band is his most current visible project. He and actor /musician (CSI:NY) Gary Sinise cofounded this classic rock group that performs internationally to include USO military shows.

Kimo lives in Chicago with singer-songwriter Carol Williams, and after 30 years of marriage they continue to collaborate creatively. They have a daughter Rebecca.